MW00657143

GUIDE TO EXPLORING

Santa Barbara with Kids

GUIDE TO EXPLORING

Santa Barbara with Kids

from tots to preteens

Annabelle Abba Brownell

Pacific Coast Publishing
Santa Barbara, California

Guide to Exploring
Santa Barbara with Kids
from tots to preteens

by Annabelle Abba Brownell

 Pacific Coast Publishing
PO Box 754
Santa Barbara, CA 93102 USA
sales@pacificcoastpub.com; www.pacificcoastpub.com

All rights reserved. No part of this book may be reproduced or transmitted in any form or by any means, electronic or mechanical, including photocopying, recording or by any information storage and retrieval system, without written permission from the author, except for the inclusion of brief quotations in a review.

Copyright © 2008 by Annabelle Abba Brownell
First Edition, 2008

Edition: Softcover
ISBN: 978-0-9815756-7-4

Published in the United States of America
Library of Congress Control Number: 2008927000

Cover and book design:
Peri Poloni-Gabriel, Knockout Design, www.knockoutbooks.com

The information in this book is presented as a guide. Every attempt has been made to confirm the accuracy of the content. Pacific Coast Publishing assumes no responsibility for errors, inaccuracies, or omissions in this book.

Dedication

~~~~~~~~~~~~~~~~~~~~~~~~~~~~~~~~~~~

For my precious family,
Peter, Hunter and Liliana,
who make my every day
an adventure.

Acknowledgements

I would like to express gratitude to the many families with whom I have had the fortune to spend time with in this Santa Barbara haven. Of those, I would like to note an extraordinary group of women who comprise the informal Montecito Playgroup. Their spirit made my landing in Santa Barbara so much more joyful. I have also had the opportunity to meet so many wonderful families in this community as my children attend local camps, classes, and school. A warm felt thanks goes to these super parents.

In addition, I was fortunate to find a local author and fellow alumnus from Thunderbird, School of Global Management. He had written a family guidebook in the past and graciously offered to edit this book. I offer my sincere gratitude to Stephen Ringler for thoroughly reviewing this guide.

Contents

~~~~~~~~~~

Kid Friendly Establishments 107

Seasonal Festivals And Activities 147

Introduction

~~~~~~~~~~~~~~~~~~~~~~~~~~~~~~~~

T he inspiration for this book came from the many parents I have had the pleasure to meet while living in this California oasis. A number of these parents have been visitors to this wonderful destination, and customers of mine at Santa Barbara Baby Company. In the name of good customer service I wanted to offer visitors a special guide to this area that focused on family friendly destinations and amenities. It is with this inspiration that I wrote this book.

Whether local or just visiting, most parents will agree that your adventure as a family is more enjoyable when you choose the most amenable establishment or activity for children. An enriched child leads to a happy parent and good experience for the whole family. With that said, choose adventures in this book which would suit your child best. A woman in my writing class shared a story with me about her first visit to Santa Barbara with her young children. Looking to have a relaxing day, she was encouraged by acquaintances to take a boat ride out to the Anacapa Islands with her children. The thought of a family boat ride on a sunny day was enticing, even more so the indulgence of a Margarita on the white sandy beach when she arrived. The reality was that the boat ride was well over an hour across rough waters with a seasick child, only to arrive on a rocky beach with no signs of commerce; not even a warm beer was an option. In response to this story, another student claimed that she had visited those same islands with her child and had a wonderful day. I present this book as a guide to help you make informed choices based on your own intuition. Add a good attitude, a sense of adventure, and perhaps a Margarita, and off you go!

About This Book

This book is offered as a practical guide to families visiting or living with children in the Santa Barbara area. All the suggestions in this book are derived from the authors own experience as well as other local parents. In the interest of impartiality, there is neither paid advertising nor paid entries in this book.

Every effort has been made to present up-to-date and accurate information in this book. Regardless, businesses and events may be discontinued or change their prices, hours, and locations. It is recommended that you call ahead of time to confirm the information. Furthermore, all the reviews made in this book are made solely by the author, and not anyone representing the respective location which is being reviewed.

The author of this book, Annabelle Abba Brownell, is owner of the Santa Barbara Baby Company, a baby and toddler equipment rental service. For travel tips about traveling with infants and toddlers, visit the web site at www.SBbabyCo.com.

Please direct input and feedback on this guidebook to sales@pacificcoastpub.com

About Santa Barbara

anta Barbara is a coastal community nestled between the
Santa Ynez Mountains and the Pacific Ocean. Hailed as
the American Riviera, Santa Barbara is 90 miles north of Los
Angeles, and 300 miles south of San Francisco. The landscape,
weather, and amenities make this an ideal location for a family
outing, as well as those looking for relaxation in the sun. In addition to enjoying days at the beach, families can bike ride, sail,
fish, kayak, play tennis, golf, camp, horseback ride, and enjoy
movies or theatre. There are festivals and events throughout
the year in the city and nearby communities.

Thriving with vibrant history, Spanish architecture, and
legendary Southern California lifestyle, Santa Barbara is
the quintessential California beach town. Boasting a lush
Mediterranean climate, a prosperous arts community, world-
class shopping and dining, and renowned wine country, Santa
Barbara is an outstanding destination.

History

Abounding in resources and natural beauty, Santa Barbara
was first discovered by the Chumash Indians. Sustained by

fish-rich waters and mountain game, the Chumash are primarily known for their fine basketry, peculiar cave paintings, and shell trade.

Portuguese explorer Juan Cabrillo laid claim to the region in the name of Spain in 1542. Sixty years later, Sebastian Vizcaino was spared his ships and lives of his crew by taking shelter in the Santa Barbara channel from a great storm. A friar on board one of the ships named the coastal landfall and bay in honor of Saint Barbara.

Two hundred years later, Father Junipero Serra founded the Santa Barbara Presidio in 1782, adding the Mission Santa Barbara four years later. The Presidios were military garrisons for the protection of missionaries established in San Diego, Santa Barbara, Monterey and San Francisco. Mission Santa Barbara is the first of three missions (including Santa Inés in Solvang and La Purísima in Lompoc) in what is now Santa Barbara County. Evidence of the Spanish influence in Santa Barbara is noticeable on her streets blooming with colorful Spanish architecture.

In 1822 the citizens of Santa Barbara swore allegiance to the Empire of Mexico ending Spanish rule in California. This rule was short-lived. In 1848 Mexico signed a treaty ceding California to the United States. Although California attained statehood in 1850, Santa Barbara retained much of its sedate pueblo atmosphere until the late 1800s, when affluent and famous visitors began arriving in great numbers.

Santa Barbara County "boomed" in the late 1800's. Streets were paved and public sewers laid. Even during the 1915-17 depression, Santa Barbara County forged ahead attracting tourists and wealthy residents from the East. This boom increased with the growth of the motion pictures industry. In 1910, the American Film Company opened Flying A Studio in the heart of Santa Barbara. This was the largest studio of its kind in the world, ultimately producing more than one thousand silent films. Although the industry eventually found its home farther south in Hollywood, movie stars had acquired a taste of this extraordinary town. They were drawn to the rich landscape and almost perfect weather, as well as the privacy and escape from the shimmer of tinsel town.

For over a century Santa Barbara has been recognized as a world-class destination. Resorts have been springing up for decades to accommodate the city's affluent guests. Ever since the era of silent films, celebrities such as Douglas Fairbanks and Mary Pickford have owned property in the area. Charlie Chaplin built the Montecito Inn in 1928, largely for visitors from Hollywood. Acquired primarily for friends and guests, Ronald Colman and Alvin Weingand bought the San Ysidro Ranch in 1935. This trend has continued to this day with many celebrities scattered throughout the coastal and mountainous neighborhoods. One can occasionally spot celebrities such as the beloved Oprah Winfrey and famous Rob Lowe in their hometown of Montecito. Julia Louis-Dreyfus and Kevin Costner have also been lured into nearby homes by the spectacular coastal lifestyle. In turn, an astounding range of successful entrepreneurs have found themselves equally attracted to the area. Ty Warner, founder of Beanie Babies, is an active resident and real estate investor, with the Ty Warner Sea Center named in his honor. It appears that the fortunate individuals who have the luxury to choose any geographical location in which to reside are drawn to Santa Barbara County.

Weather

Santa Barbara has over 300 days of sun per year. The climate is mild with very low humidity. Annual precipitation averages approximate 16 inches and occurs mostly between December and March. The average annual rainfall is only 18 inches, which is comparable to many desert communities.

For 40 miles, the Santa Barbara coastline runs almost due East/West. This alignment moderates the ocean currents that flow past Santa Barbara. The nearby mountains are relatively close to the ocean and provide protection from the inland heat as well as winter storms. A chain of islands starting 20 miles off shore breaks that force of ocean storms as well.

The year-round average temperature is a comfortable 62 degrees. As such, there is no off-season in Santa Barbara.

Month	Average High	Average Low	Average Inches of Rainfall
January	67	43	4.3
February	71	46	3.8
March	66	44	2.3
April	70	50	1.5
May	69	52	.5
June	71	55	.1
July	75	57	.05
August	77	61	.1
September	76	58	.3
October	73	52	.4
November	75	52	2.2
December	68	51	2.5

The best combination of temperature and outside activities is usually considered to be from June through October. However, the winter season in Santa Barbara is exceptionally mild with a combination of sunny days and invigorating temperatures. During the months of December through April, many visitors flock to Santa Barbara from colder climates in North America, and Europe.

Santa Barbara Neighborhoods

The Waterfront

Regarded as one of the most beautiful coastlines in the country, the Santa Barbara waterfront is complete with its' scenic Harbor and Wharf. Stroll from East to West Beach and absorb the Pacific setting and social activity. Along the way, you will encounter parks, restaurants, shops, bike trails, and coastal landscape. Running from noon until sunset every half hour, the Waterfront Shuttle runs continuously along this coastline. Cabrillo Boulevard is the quintessential California beach strand. It is great for strolling or biking with the family. There are activities and rental services along the coast. Older kids can skateboard at Skaters Point, located at the beach, just east of Stearns Wharf. Chase Palm Park has a wonderful playground, gardens with long stretches of grass, picnic tables and a pond. There is a classic, wood-carved grand carousel that operates daily. Families enjoy concerts here every Thursday night during the summer.

The Harbor

The Harbor is home to both yachts and fishing boats. There are many options for water adventure including kayak and jet ski rental, sailing and boat excursions, as well as whale watching trips. The restaurants are fun and plentiful. Visit the discovery section for kids at the Maritime Museum. Follow the walking path to the far end of the harbor where you will find a sand bar for lounging. Kids will get a kick out of watching all the boats pass by or the fisherman offload their daily catch of fish and squid.

Downtown

Downtown Santa Barbara hosts a variety of retailers from national to unique local specialty shops. The Spanish-Mediterranean architecture features outdoor paseos, beautifully landscaped plazas, and brick-lined sidewalks. Enjoy casual or fine dining and a variety of cultural venues including galleries, performing arts, historic sites and museums. A Red Tile Map at the Visitors Center on Garden Street and Cabrillo offers a self-guided tour of this area.

Mission District

Perhaps the bud that gave bloom to the Spanish-influenced architecture in the area, the Mission Santa Barbara sits majestically in the heart of the Mission District. A visit to the nearby Museum of Natural History and Botanical Gardens will give you an additional glimpse into the areas storied past.

Riviera

Touted as the 'American Riviera', Santa Barbara is likened to its European counterpart because of this region. Its temperate climate and East-West coastal orientation allow for day-long southerly sun to shine upon this region, and down on the shores and cityscape below. One drive up these panoramic hillsides and you will immediately feel the magnificence of this ocean-perched locale. With the sun-shining and a clear view, you will find it difficult to return to where you came from.

Uptown

Generally visited for shopping purposes, upper State Street is festooned by clusters of retail merchants. La Cumbre Plaza is a large shopping mall anchored by two department stores, Macys and Sears, and more than 60 shops, restaurants, services and easy parking. There is also a Farmers Market every Wednesday.

Neighboring Communities

Carpinteria

About 10 minutes south of the city of Santa Barbara, is this delightful California beach town – casual, friendly and inviting. Downtown is lined with mom and pop stores, taquerias and burger joints. Most people stroll leisurely around town in shorts, T-shirts and sandals. The beach is extensive, and a wonderful experience for families. It is considered one of safest beaches along the Pacific Coast due to the extended shallow waters. Spend a day in Carpinteria when you would like a fun, family beach day and stroll.

Montecito

This township is adjacent to Santa Barbara. It is a lush coastal community filled with elegant landscapes and great Mediterranean estates. Visit the safe and clean beaches, upscale shops, and great restaurants.

Summerland

This quaint seaside village is nestled on a hillside overlooking the Pacific Ocean. It is a popular attraction for antique shoppers and surfers alike. Many come here on weekends to enjoy the friendly cafes and quiet beaches.

Goleta

Descended from a rich farming and ranching industry, Goleta has grown into a family-oriented community. It was best known as the top lemon producing region in the country and still hosts the Annual Lemon Festival. You'll find excellent golf facilities, including the renowned coastal Sandpiper Golf Course, as well as the venerated Bacara Resort. The esteemed University of California, Santa Barbara (UCSB) sits along the coastline in a small section of town called Isla Vista, and brings to it an academic stimulus.

Santa Ynez Valley

Santa Ynez Valley is comprised of six communities: Ballard, Buellton, Los Alamos, Los Olivos, Santa Ynez village, and Solvang. It is recognized for its' celebrated wineries. In addition to the 50 world-class wineries, visitors can go hiking, biking, fishing, boating or visit a horse farm. Cachuma Lake is a popular destination for families wanting to get outdoors, as is Solvang (Little Denmark) which claims over 300 stores, charming bakeries and restaurants.

Ojai

Tucked away in the valley beyond, Ojai is widely identified for being an active art community, spa retreat and spiritual sanctuary. The serenity of the environment is alluring, and the services and amenities cater to the laid back ambiance.

Ventura & Oxnard

Most families are drawn to the coastal elements of both the Ventura and Oxnard areas. The beaches are active, expansive, and the sunsets are spectacular. The Ventura Harbor Village and Channel Islands Harbor feature lively marinas, enjoyable shops and restaurants, as well as seasonal activities for the kids.

Transportation

Transportation options in Santa Barbara can be inexpensive due to the relative proximity of most destinations in the town and vicinity. If you are traveling with young children under 6 years in age, a rental car may be your best option due to car seat requirements.

Santa Barbara Airport (SBA):

Options from the airport include rental cars, taxi and limousine services, and airport shuttles. The airport hosts national rental agencies with offices adjacent to the terminal. Taxis can be hailed just outside the terminal as well. See the phone numbers at the end of this section for local transportation companies. Some hotels offer a free shuttle service from the airport - check with the hotel directly for details. For a door-to-door airport shuttle, contact Super Ride at (805) 683-9636 or Roadrunner at 800-247-7919.

To/From Los Angeles Airport (LAX):

The best options are a rental car from LAX or the Santa Barbara Airbus, a daily shuttle that operates between Santa Barbara and LAX. For the Airbus, visit www.SantaBarbaraAirbus.com or call (805) 964-7759

To/From Burbank Airport:

The best options are a rental car or the Amtrak train which travels directly from Santa Barbara to Burbank Airport. The Pacific Surfliner is the Amtrak line you will be riding. Visit www.amtrak.com for more details or call 1-800-872-7245

Rental Cars

Airport Agencies	Reservation Number	Terminal Number
Avis	800.831.2847	805.964.4848
Budget	800.527.0700	805.967.1202
Hertz	800.654.3131	805.967.0411
National	800.227.7368	805.967.1202
Alamo	800.462.5266	805.967.1202
Off-Airport Agencies	Reservation Number	Local Number
Enterprise	800-736-8222	805.683.0067
Thrifty	800-847-4389	805.681.1222

Taxicabs	Reservation Number
American Cab	(805) 689-0683
Allen Simmons Taxi	(805) 331-3159
Blue Dolphin Cab	(805) 964-7888
Beachside Taxi	(805) 963-0412
Fiesta Taxi	(805) 895-5555
Gold Cab Taxi	(805) 681-9000
Rose Cab	(805) 564-2600
Rockstar Cab*	(805) 451-9999
Santa Barbara Airport Cab	(805) 895-2422
Santa Barbara Checker Cab	(805) 560-8284
Scenic Tours Taxi	(805) 403-5466
Seaside Taxi	(805) 565-3002
Yellow Cab	(805) 965-5111

*Rockstar Cab claims to have a "10,000 Song iPod in every cab"—perhaps one song is a lullaby?

Limousines	Reservation Number
JLS Transportation	(805) 961-9111
Limousine Link & Sedan Service	(805) 898-9506
Luxury By Day	(805) 965-6869
Nite Owl Limousine Service	(805) 383-0214
Rockstar Limousine	(805) 451-9999
Santa Barbara Limousine	(805) 964-5466
Shasta Limousine Service	(805) 452-3976
Spencer's Limousine & Tours	(805) 884-9700

Special Needs:

If you are traveling with a senior or passenger who is disabled, try EasyLift. They are available from dawn to late night and can accommodate an extra companion with the disabled passenger as well.

Contact Info: (805) 681-1181

www.EasyLift.org

Other Local Shuttles

Downtown Shuttle and Waterfront Shuttle

These shuttles operate all day long with pick-ups every 10 to 30 minutes. Look for a turquoise and white colored electric shuttle bus running along Cabrillo Boulevard and along downtown State Street. The kids will enjoy the ride and it's an inexpensive adventure for only 25 cents. Ask the driver for a free shuttle transfer upon boarding your first shuttle – you can use it for your next ride.

Contact Info: www.sbmtd.gov (See Waterfront Shuttle)

For a complete guide to traveling Santa Barbara without a car, go to the web site below. Order a car free map online and receive transportation discounts too!

Contact Info: www.SantaBarbaraCarFree.com

Emergency Contacts

EMERGENCY	911
FIRE	(805) 965-5254 Santa Barbara City (805) 969-7762 Montecito (805) 684-4591 Summerland (805) 684-4591 Carpinteria (805) 681-5500 Goleta
POLICE	(805) 897-2300 Santa Barbara City (805) 684-4561 Montecito (805) 684-4561 Summerland (805) 684-4561 Carpinteria (805) 681-4100 Goleta
California Missing Childrens Hotline	1-800-222-3463
Coast Guard Search and Rescue	1-800-221-8724
Poison Control Center	1-800-222-1222
Santa Barbara Cottage Hospital- Outpatient	1-(805) 682-7111
Children's Medical Clinic	1-(805) 965-1095 1-(805) 564-2532 After Hours
Pediatric Dental Practice	1-(805) 963-4404

Car Seat Installation

The County Fire Stations offer to check your car seat installation free of charge. Call the Santa Barbara County Fire Department Injury Prevention Hotline, 681-5550 x5532. The county offers a monthly two-hour presentation to the public as well. Please call the number above for more information.

Local Attractions

F or a complete selection of local attractions and activities in the Santa Barbara area, you can visit one of the following tourist centers. They are staffed by local residents and can offer personalized suggestions. Call them first to verify hours and directions.

Santa Barbara Visitors Center

Contact Info: 1 Garden Street and Cabrillo, Santa Barbara
(805) 965-3021
www.sbchamber.org

Outdoors Santa Barbara Visitor Center

Contact Info: 113 Harbor Way, Santa Barbara
(805) 884-1475

Ocean-Fun activities or education are noted by the following icon:

Historical Attractions

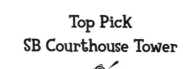

Top Pick
SB Courthouse Tower

Casa de la Guerra

A wonderful museum with some fabulous vignettes located next to de la Guerra Plaza.

Hours: Thu-Sun 12-4

Cost: $3 Ages 16 and up

Contact Info: 15 E De La Guerra Street, Santa Barbara
(805) 966-6961
www.sbthp.org/casa.htm

El Presidio de Santa Barbara

The last of four military fortresses built by the Spanish along the wild coastal frontier, this compound is a working archeological dig. Catch a tour with a docent who will avidly share the lifestyle of those who inhabited this region in another era. Special Family Craft Days, and "Presidio Pastimes" Family Days are held throughout the year.

Hours: Daily 10:30-4:30

Cost: $3 Ages 16 and up (Free with Casa De La Guerra entry)

Contact Info: 123 E Canon Perdido Street, Santa Barbara
(805) 965-0093
www.sbthp.org/presidio.htm

Mission Santa Barbara

The Mission is the central historical landmark in the city, for it marks the seminal landing of the Spaniards in Santa Barbara and their strong influence in this county. Upon approach, you will be awed by the unique façade nestled below the palm shaded setting and Santa Ynez Mountains. Children are immediately drawn to the majestic water fountain, long concrete trough, cactus garden, and lawn area that adorn the entrance. Take a short tour for an historical overview. The cemetery in the back of the mission hosts many fascinating ancient crypts for the young onlooker. Bring a picnic to enjoy in the Rose Garden across the street when it is in full bloom.

Hours: Daily 9-5

Cost: Free except Tours ($4/adult, $1/children over 6-11)

Contact Info: 2201 Laguna St, Santa Barbara
(805) 682-4713
www.santabarbaramission.org

 ## SB Courthouse Tower

For a sweeping 360° view of the city, the Channel Islands, and the Santa Ynez Mountains visit each quarter of the tower viewing platform. Here you will find a descriptive map of each panorama you are viewing. The architecture of the building is elegant and just outside the Courthouse is the Sunken Gardens which hosts festivals and concerts throughout the year.

Hours: M-F 8-5, Sat & Sun 10-4:30 (Tours at 2pm daily)

Cost: Free

Contact Info: 1100 Anacapa Street, Santa Barbara
(805) 962-6464
www.santabarbaracourthouse.org

Santa Barbara Historical Museum

Not your typical quiet, indoor museum. This location has outdoor components, as well as educational materials such as photos, maps, books and manuscripts.

Hours: Tue-Sun, closed Mondays.

Cost: Free

Contract Info: 136 E De la Guerra Street, Santa Barbara
(805) 966-1601
www.santabarbaramuseum.com

Carpinteria Valley Historical Museum

Although small in size, this museum provides a fascinating glimpse into the Valley's past through artifacts, photographs, and special exhibits. It also hosts arts & crafts faires, school tours and children's programs.

Hours: Tue-Sat 1-4pm

Cost: Free

Contact Info: 956 Maple Avenue, Carpinteria
(805) 684-3112
www.carpinteriahistoricalmuseum.org

Goleta Valley Historical Society

Rancho La Patera is home to the historic Stow House, and associated museums. Look for community events held on these historical grounds.

Hours: Sat & Sun 2 - 4pm

Cost: Free, except tours ($5/adult)

Contact Info: 304 N Los Carneros, Goleta
(805) 681-7216
www.goletahistory.org

Educational Exploration

Top Pick
Ty Warner Sea Center

Arroyo Burro Watershed

The Watershed Resource Center provides an opportunity for kids to experience our environment first-hand by testing water samples and studying them in the wet lab, using an interactive watershed model to understand sources of pollution, and taking guided interpretive walks along the nearby Arroyo Burro creek and beach.

Hours: Under new managment — Call for hours of operation.

Cost: Free

Contact Info: 2981 Cliff Drive, Santa Barbara
(805) 682-6113
www.artfromscrap.org/wrc_index.html

Astronomy Programs at the Santa Barbara Museum of Natural History

Daily and monthly shows include views through the telescope in the Gladwin Planetarium in the Santa Barbara. Many shows are tailored for the younger audience. There are also exclusive evening shows held throughout the month.

Hours: Vary, see web site or call

Cost: Museum Members FREE;
non-members $4.00-$6.00/person

Contact Info: 2559 Puesta del Sol Road, Santa Barbara
(805) 682-4711
www.sbnature.org/education/planetarium

Channel Islands Marine Floating Lab

For an educational experience for the whole family, try 3 1/2 hours on-board a marine lab wherein participants are able to analyze the biological, chemical and physical properties of the ocean. Participants learn about marine animal specimens, plankton and other microscopic organisms. The staff sets up a program tailored towards specific age groups, from Kindergarten to adults. Participants rotate through stations taking part in hands-on learning experiences. The boat holds up to 40 persons, and you must reserve the whole lab per party, no matter the number of participants.

Hours: Call

Cost: $475.00 for 40 persons & 3 1/2 hours.

Contact Info: 4151 South Victoria Avenue, Oxnard
(805) 382-4563
www.floatinglab.com

Research Experience and Education Facility – the REEF

UCSB Marine Science Institute opens its doors for visits to its research aquarium and touch tanks. Children of all ages will delight in this educational experience, and the staff is exceptionally knowledgeable and friendly. The facility is usually open year round, although hours will vary seasonally so call ahead. The REEF is adjacent to the shoreline as well, so bring your beach gear too.

Hours: Saturdays from 11am-2pm

Cost: Free

Contact Info: Marine Science Institute, University of California,
Santa Barbara (UCSB) Campus, Goleta
(805) 893-8765
www.msi.ucsb.edu (click on "education" link)

Santa Barbara County Library Storytimes

Storytimes are held for children ages 3 to 5 years old and may include stories, poems, finger plays, and music. There are a variety of storytelling venues offered throughout the area that are sponsored by the Santa Barbara Public Library System.

Hours: Generally Tue-Thur around 10:30am

Cost: Free

Contact Info: Santa Barbara Central Library
(805) 962-7653
www.sbplibrary.org (see Hours and Location link for libraries within the county)

 ### Ty Warner Sea Center

Ty Warner Sea Center is a fun, engaging, interactive marine education facility located on Stearns Wharf. It is owned and operated by the Santa Barbara Museum of Natural History. At the center you will find interactive exhibits sampling and testing ocean water, studying animal behavior, and examining microscopic marine life. There are live tide pool animal encounters and a theater showcasing the wonders of the Santa Barbara Channel. Check the events calendar as there are many special activities hosted for children. Kids marvel at the full-size model of a gray whale suspended overhead, be sure to point it out!

Hours: 10am to 5pm daily

Cost: Adults $7, Seniors (65 and over) $6, Teens $6, Children $4 , Children under 2 free

Local Attractions

Contact Info: 211 Stearns Wharf, Santa Barbara
(805) 962-2526
www.sbnature.org / seacenter

Whiz Kidz

At Whiz Kidz children enjoy learning through the use of the latest computer games and programs on the PC, Mac or XBOX. They can also surf the Internet and use the color printer. Kids can be dropped off to play and be supervised by the Whiz Kidz team, or parents can stay and play too. Free preschool story time – call for hours.

Hours: M-Thur 2-7pm, Fri 2-9pm, Sat 5-9pm, Sun 1-6pm

Cost: hourly rate of $7-$10

Contact Info: 189 Turnpike Road, Suite A, Santa Barbara
(805) 696-9449
www.whizkidz.net

Carpinteria State Beach Visitors Center

Small in size, this center houses an indoor tide pool maintained by volunteers. Come here to learn more about this region and the Native American culture that resided centuries ago on this coastline.

Hours: Vary Seasonally

Cost: Free

Contact Info: Carpinteria State Beach, Carpinteria
(805) 684-2811
www.parks.ca.gov

Museums

┌─────────────────────────────────┐
│   **Top Pick**   │
│   **Santa Barbara Museum of**   │
│   **Natural History**   │
│   │
└─────────────────────────────────┘

Carriage Museum

Located in Pershing Park near the waterfront, this museums' collection consists of mud wagons, an army wagon, a circus wagon, and 20 others. There are over 50 saddles once belonging to famous people, such as Cisco Kid, Will Rogers, and Clark Gable.

Hours: Daily 9-3

Cost: Free

Contact Info: 129 Castillo Street
(805) 962-2353
www.carriagemuseum.org

Santa Barbara Maritime Museum

The size of this museum makes it a quick and manageable visit. The location is adjacent to the harbor so the boat watching adds to the experience. There is a special discovery section for kids, a periscope, a collection of ship models and more. Be sure to a get a free kids treasure map and visit the museum store.

Hours: Summer 10-6, Winter 10-5

Costs: $6 adults, $4 Youth, $1 children

Contact Info: 113 Harbor Way, Suite 190, Santa Barbara
(805) 962-8404 ext.115
www.sbmm.org

Santa Barbara Museum of Art

Perfect for a short visit while you are downtown, this museum has a special Children's Gallery. After your viewing, visit the Museum of Art Store for a unique selection of imaginative and artistic toys.

Hours: Tue-Sun 11-5

Cost: $9 Adults, $6 Ages 6-17, Under 6 free

Contact Info: 1130 State Street, Santa Barbara
(805) 884.6454
www.sbma.net

 ## Santa Barbara Museum of Natural History

Exhibits feature mammals, birds, fish, reptiles, plant life and geology of the Pacific Coast and Channel Islands as well as prehistoric Native American life. This is home to the only full sized Pygmy Mammoth skeleton anywhere in the world. There is also a planetarium onsite with hands-on space exhibits as well as shows. Hourly, daily and weekly children's workshops are offered throughout the year. Don't miss the life-size blue whale skeleton near the entrance of the museum – the kids are always fascinated and it may turn it out to be the main attraction for them.

Hours: Daily 10-5

Cost: $8 Adults, $7 Youth 13-17, $5 Children 2-12, Under 2 free

Contact Info: 2559 Puesta Del Sol Road, Santa Barbara
(805) 682-4711
www.sbnature.org

Susan Quinlan Doll and Teddy Bear Museum and Library

One of the largest displays of dolls and teddy bears in the United States. California's rich heritage of doll and teddy bear artists and manufacturers, as well as the influences of Santa Barbara artists and celebrities on the doll world are recognized. Come and relive your childhood memories and share those memories with your children and grandchildren. The gift shop offers a variety of dolls, teddy bears, books, and related collectibles. Call for museum hour changes and closures.

Hours: Fri, Sat, Sun, Mon 11-5

Cost: $6.50 Adults, $3.50 Pre-teens

Contact Info: 122 West Canon Perdido Street, Santa Barbara
(805) 730-1707
www.quinlanmuseum.com

Fun In The Sun

Top Pick
Santa Barbara Zoo

Antique Carousel at Chase Palm Park

One of the highlights of the Chase Palm Park is the carousel, which is protected from the beachfront climate by a beautiful carousel housing structure. The carousel was carved by Allan Hershell in 1919. It is 40 feet in diameter, has 36 intricately carved horses and two chariots and is a magnificent example of carousel carving at its pinnacle.

Hours: Varies Seasonally

Cost: $2 per ride

Contact Info: 223 E Cabrillo Blvd, Santa Barbara
(805)963-9463

Fairview Gardens

The Center for Urban Agriculture at Fairview Gardens provides the community with fresh, chemical-free fruits and vegetables, and educational programs for the whole family. Families are welcome to tour the farm any day.

Hours: 10am-6pm

Cost: Free

Contact Info: 598 N. Fairview Avenue, Goleta
(805) 967-7369
www.fairviewgardens.org

Santa Barbara Zoological Gardens

The most frequented attraction for children in the area. A beautifully landscaped and compact zoo filled with a variety of animals. It is the perfect size to visit for just a morning or afternoon and still enjoy it in its entirety. There are play areas for the children, lawns for picnics, a train ride and petting area. The location is picturesque overlooking a 42-acre saltwater lagoon and bird refuge on one side, and the Pacific Ocean on the other. Visit the lagoon across the street to feed the ducks after your zoo visit. Rent a bike or surrey and ride down Cabrillo Avenue to the zoo then ride back after your visit. It is a wonderfully entertaining excursion for the family and won't take longer than 1-3 hours.

Hours: Open 10:00 a.m. - 5:00 p.m. every day

Cost: Adults 13-59: $10 Children 2-12/Seniors 60+: $8
Children under 2: Free

Parking: $3 (free with SB Zoo Membership)

Contact Info: 500 Niños Drive, Santa Barbara
(805) 962-5339
www.sbzoo.org

Santa Barbara Botanic Garden

78 acres of exquisite exhibits of California native plants set in beautifully designed landscapes. Explore the miniature plant life environments, from desert-like cactus gardens to ponds filled with turtles and fish. Over 5 miles of trails meander across the canyon walls of the garden. On a hot day the Mission Creek is a pleasurable location to splash around with the kids, complete with a dam and small waterfall intact from the old missionary days. Those not looking to get wet can try climbing the enormous boulders in the garden ... one even has a small cave at it's base! Look on their online calendar for their monthly kids events. Don't forget to ask for the special Detective booklet for kids – it guides them through a tour and activities in the garden while solving a mystery.

Hours: March - October: 9:00 a.m. to 6:00 p.m.
November - February: 9:00 a.m. to 5:00 p.m.

Cost: $8.00 Adults, $6.00 Seniors (60+ years),
$6.00 children 13-17, $4.00 Children 2-12 years ,
Children under 2 free

Contact Info: 1212 Mission Canyon Rd, Santa Barbara
(805) 682-4726
www.sbbg.org

Local Attractions

Santa Barbara Polo Games

Santa Barbara has a lengthy history associated with the game of polo. The Santa Barbara Polo Club welcomes visitors for Sunday games from April through October. Bring a picnic if you like.

Hours: 1:00pm and 3:00pm games

Cost: $10 per ticket

Contact Info: 3375 Foothill Road, Carpinteria
(805) 684-6683
www.sbpolo.com

Santa Barbara Water Taxi

This Lil' Toot shuttles people between the harbor and Stearns Wharf over 12 times on a daily basis. The ride is no longer than 10 minutes each way. The staff is very friendly and especially accommodating with children. Kids get to drive the boat and receive a sticker badge for being a 'Junior Captain'. You don't need reservations, just find their kiosk at the wharf or harbor and wait for the next boat. This is a personal favorite of ours as children get to experience a boat ride in a short time frame for just $1. Take the round trip for an added bonus!

Hours: Winter 12pm-Sunset, Summer 10am-Sunset

Cost: $1 child, $2 adult each way

Contact Info: Catch at The Harbor or Stearns Wharf
(805) 896-6900
www.sbwatertaxi.com

Stearns Wharf

California's oldest operating wharf, and Santa Barbara's most visited landmark. Children can touch marine life at the Ty Warner Sea Center. Watch the pelicans and early morning fishing boats arriving with their catch, as well as the fishermen on the pier catching mackeral and sometimes salmon. Narrated coastal cruises depart from the wharf on a regular basis. Stearn Wharf's charming ice cream and candy shops are always a lure for the kids. For a free marine life viewing, check out the live fish and crustaceans in the tanks at Santa Barbara Shellfish Company.

Contact Info: End of State Street
www.stearnswharf.org

Energetic Outlets

Batty's Bat-A-Way

Batting cages for softball and baseball, as well as a tiny arcade.

Hours: M-F 11-9, Weekends 10-8

Cost: $2.50/token (1 token = 19 pitches)

Contact Info: 226 S. Milpas Street, Santa Barbara
(805) 962-6666

El Capitan Ranch Horseback Riding & Chuck Wagon Dinners

In addition to horseback riding lessons, this ranch offers a Chuck Wagon Dinner ride. Every Friday night, a tractor drawn hay wagon ride will deliver you to a working horse ranch where the family can enjoy horse shoe pits, cowboy roping, carriage rides, live entertainment, and a camp fire. Dinner is included.

Contact Info: 10920 Calle Real, Santa Barbara -
(805)685-1147
www.elcapranch.com

Frisbee Course at Evergreen Park

This free 18-hole disc (Frisbee) course is open to the public. Print out a map and scorecard at the web site below.

Contact Info: Brandon and Evergreen Drives, Goleta
(805) 681-5650
www.members.cox.net/evergreen/frameset1.htm

Skater's Point

14,600 square feet of skateboard and in-line fun, this state-of-the-art cement facility features a half-pipe, rails, fun boxes and other skating elements. Younger and less experienced skaters are encouraged to skate on weekends before noon, especially Saturday morning. Helmets, elbow and knee pads required at all times. Need Gear? Call nearby Santa Barbara Skate Shop at (805) 899-8669.

Hours: 8am to 1/2 hour after sunset.

Cost: Free

Contact Info: Cabrillo Boulevard at Garden Street
(805) 564-5418
www.santabarbaraca.gov/Parks

Zodos Bowling and Beyond

The retro décor and fun atmosphere make this bowling alley a hit with kids. Special consideration is made for the young bowlers with bumpers in the lanes upon request. The arcade is an added bonus where kids collect tickets at each game and trade them for prizes, much the same as Chuck E. Cheese. The grill is exceptionally good and is an added bonus to the whole excursion. Perfect for that rare rainy day in Santa Barbara.

Hours: 8:30am until late night,
except M - Thur from 5:30pm - 9pm

Cost: $22-$28 per hour per lane, or $4 -$5.50 per person per game

Contact Info: 5925 Calle Real, Goleta
(805) 967-0128
www.zodobowl.com

Oxnard Ice

Our town is not well known for winter sports. As such, if you are looking to indulge in an ice sport, you will have to drive to Oxnard to take a spin around an ice skating rink.

Hours: M-F 12-11pm, Sat & Sun 8am-11pm

Contact Info: 830 Wagon Wheel Road, Oxnard
(805)988-4440
www.oxnardice.com

Skating Plus

If roller skating is your interest, and you are seeking a controlled environment or lessons, then drive on down to Ventura. Here you will find a clean and safe environment for both inline and roller skating.

Hours: Call for schedule or visit web site

Contact Info: 1720 Mesa Verde Ave. Ventura
(805) 656-2120
www.skatingplus.com

Local Attractions

Arts And Crafts

· ·

```
Top Pick
Art From Scrap
```

2000 Degrees

Kids of all ages have a great time painting in this safe and creative atmosphere. They are especially proud to take home their special ceramic keepsake. Choose from over 200 pieces of bisqueware and 60 color hues to paint. After you have painted it, your ceramic creation will be glazed and fired in the kilns on site.

Hours: T-F 12-8, Sat 10-9, Sun 12-6

Cost: $5 plus cost of ceramic piece

Contact Info: 1206 State Street, Santa Barbara
(805) 882-1817

 Art From Scrap

Art Workshops led by local artists are held every Saturday morning for kids of all ages. No reservation necessary - just show up and have fun with creativity.

Hours: Saturday Workshops from 10-11:30am

Cost: $6 Kids, $10 Adults

Contact Info: 302 E. Cota, Santa Barbara
(866) 884-0459x13
www.artfromscrap.org

Color Me Mine

This international franchise is known for being a relaxing, inviting space with warm, natural wood furniture and shelves, contemporary music, providing an intimate environment. All the paints and glazes are lead free, 100% friendly to the environment and completely safe for kids and adults. See their web site for special events.

Hours: M-Thur 11-9, Fri 11-11, Sat 10-11

Cost: $6/kid, $9.50/adult plus cost of ceramic piece

Contact Info: 7044 Market Place Drive, Goleta
(805) 571-1601
www.goleta.colormemine.com

Santa Barbara Arts and Crafts Show

Inspired by the sidewalk art shows of Europe and the prestigious "Jardin del Arte" in Mexico City, this showcase features artists and vendors solely from Santa Barbara County. In addition to original drawings, paintings, graphics, sculpture, crafts and photography, you will find many unique children selections such as toys, dolls, tents, clothing and artwork.

Hours: All weekend during high tourist seasons.

Cost: Free

Contact Info: 1118 East Cabrillo Boulevard, Santa Barbara
(805) 897-1982
www.sbaacs.com

Theater

Ensemble Theatre Company's Storybook Theatre

Familiar and endearing children's plays are staged seasonally by this performance troop. See the Storybook page on their web site.

Contact Info: (805) 962-8606
www.ensembletheatre.com

PCPA (Pacific Conservatory of the Performing Arts) Theaterfest

Seasonal selections of children's classics are performed from Disney to Seuss. See their Student Matinee page on the web site under the Educational section. Performances are held both in Solvang and Santa Maria.

Contact Info: (805) 922-8313
www.PCPA.org

Performances to Grow On

These performances encompass a variety of artistic and cultural traditions that are educational, imaginative, and engaging. A treat for all ages. Choose from a variety of performances at different locations in the area.

Contact Info: 201 Park Road, Ojai
(805) 646-8907
www.ptgo.org

Movies & Me

Grab your stroller, diaper bag, and child and head down to the Camino Real Theatre. The first Tuesday of each month at 10am is dedicated especially to parents with infants. You can view any of the movies playing in that theatre at that hour with the comfort of knowing that the theater will be full of moms with toddlers. Full disruptions allowed!

Contact Info: 7040 Marketplace Drive, Goleta
(805) 963-9503
www.metrotheatres.com

The Great Outdoors

Playgrounds

Most all the parks have BBQ facilities either adjacent or nearby the playground, and there are almost always picnic tables and restrooms as well. Take advantage of the local climate and bring along charcoal and a few burgers, then settle down for a while. It doesn't take much more in Santa Barbara to create the perfect afternoon.

PARK PLAYGROUNDS

**Top Pick
Chase Palm Park**

For more information about parks in the area, please visit the following web sites:

City of SB Parks & Recreation
(805) 564-5418
www.sbparksandrecreation.com

County of Santa Barbara Parks
(805) 568-2461
www.sbparks.com

Isla Vista Parks and Recreation
(805) 968-2017
www.ivparks.org

Goleta Parks and Recreation
(805) 967-4618
www.goletavalley.com

City of Carpinteria Parks and Recreation
(805) 684-5405
www.carpinteria.ca.us/parks_rec

Park Playgrounds	Location	Features	Comments
Alameda Park – Kids World	1400 Santa Barbara St Micheltorena & Garden	9 acre tree-shaded park with enormous castle-like wooden play structure and mosaic covered walls, complete with concrete whale and dolphin for climbing. Smaller toddler area as well.	Near downtown State Street Cross the street to visit Alice Keck botanical garden and pond
Chase Palm Park	223 E. Cabrillo Blvd Across from Beach, near Garden St.	Colorful and unique play structures with a coastal theme. Complete with concrete whale statue that spouts during summer season. Large antique carousel operates daily. Plaza and pond meander through the park.	Near Stearns Wharf
Elings Park	298 Las Positas Road (805) 569-5611	An enormous non-profit park. Preschool & toddler sized play structures. Several hiking trails meander around the undeveloped portions of the park. BMX track for the dirt bikers – helmets mandatory.	Dog-friendly area with many dogs off-leash. Movie nights and Family Overnight Camping events during Summer season.

The Great Outdoors

Park Playgrounds	Location	Features	Comments
Oak Park	300 W. Alamar Ave. Alamar & Junipero (805) 564-5418	Creekside park with a big play structure for older kids and separate toddler playground. Water fountains and wading pool operate in the summer. Bonus amenities include tennis courts, dancing stage, horseshoe pit.	Kids enjoy exploring the bridge that crosses the creek. Venue for seasonal cultural festivals throughout the year.
Tuckers Grove	805 San Antonio Creek Road (805) 967-1112	Large open spaces with 2 playgrounds, volleyball, horseshoe pits, ball fields, bike and hiking trails leading up into the hills.	Bring your Hot Wheel cars for the cement race track designed for racing little hot rods
Stevens Park	258 Canon Drive (805) 564-5418	25 acre creekside park with a play structure and hik-ing trails.	
La Mesa Park	295 Meigs Rd.	Gently rolling hills with large grass areas – with ocean views; kids love to explore nearby wooded area. Relatively large play structure and sandbox.	Across from the popular Lazy Acres market – with wonderful take-out picnic food.

Park Playgrounds	Location	Features	Comments
Rocky Nook Park	610 Mission Canyon Road (805) 681-5650	Large creekside park speckled with large sandstone boulders. Encircled by oaks, the playground is deeper in the park. Beyond the playground is a short, circular hiking path. Horseshoe pit is an added bonus.	Across the main road from the Museum of Natural History & the Santa Barbara Mission.
Stow Grove Park	580 La Patera Lane, Goleta (805) 964-2311	Situated among groves of redwood trees, sycamores, oaks and eucalyptus. Large play structure, volleyball courts, baseball field, horseshoe pits and a field for croquet or miniature golf.	Bring your croquet or golf equipment!
Anisq'Oyo' Park	950 Embarcadero Del Mar Isla Vista near UCSB	3.17 acre park with a rustic windmill, a large pond, an amphitheater, and children's play structure.	Kids love the freshwater pond that is home to ducks, egrets, herons, frogs, turtles, fish and other wildlife.
Toro Canyon Park	576 Toro Canyon Road (805) 969-3315	Enormous secluded park in a large canyon setting. In addition to a play structure, there are horseshoes, volleyball, hiking and bike trails.	

The Great Outdoors

Park Playgrounds	Location	Features	Comments
Heath Ranch Park	Eucalyptus Lane, Carpinteria (off El Carro Road) (805) 684-5405	Neighborhood park and historic landmark. Huge tree trunks for climbing. Adobe house ruins. Play Structure and expansive lawn.	No Restrooms.

BEACH PLAYGROUNDS

**Top Pick
Lookout Park**

Beach Playgrounds	Location	Features	Comments
East Beach Playground	1118 E. Cabrillo Blvd.	Nice play structure located directly on the beach. Adjacent to casual East Beach Grill for snacks or meal. Close to the pier and next to Bike Path	Wonderful pancake breakfast at the Beach Grill.
Goleta Beach Park	5986 Sandspit Road, Goleta (805) 967-1300	Beachside Play Structure near bike trails, horseshoe pit, and volleyball. Close to the pier and next to Bike Path.	Try the Beachside Grill for lunch or dinner. There is also a take-out option next to the Grill.

Beach Playgrounds	Location	Features	Comments
📢 **Lookout Park**	Evans Avenue at the beach in Summerland	Scenic ocean bluff setting with substantial play structure. Horseshoe and volleyball courts also.	
West Beach Park	401 Shoreline Drive	Conveniently located between the pier and the harbor. Small playground and wading pool. Wading pool open May-September with an on-duty lifeguard. Next to Bike Path.	Try the nearby harbor for breakfast or lunch at the water's edge
Shoreline Park	Shoreline Drive at Santa Rosa Drive	Scenic ocean bluff park with dramatic views of harbor, Channel Islands & Santa Ynez mountains. Nice playgrounds and grass areas. Trail along bluff for walking or skating. Beach access via stairs with Tidal pool area during low tide. Bike path nearby.	No Shade

The Great Outdoors

The Best Beaches

. . . .

The selected beaches below offer the best choice for a family visit. Special consideration is given to availability of restroom facilities, easy access to the beach, food options nearby and surf conditions. Dogs are not allowed on city or state beaches, although they are allowed on county beaches with a leash.

Top Pick
Carpinteria Beach

Beach	Location	Features	Comments
Goleta Beach Park	Sandspit Road (off Ward Memorial Blvd), Goleta	Expansive beach with large playground. Palm trees, grassy lawns and BBQ facilities. Beachside Snack Bar and Grill.	Go fishing at nearby Goleta Beach Pier. Bring your bikes and ride along the bike path.
Arroyo Burro	Cliff Drive at Las Positas Road, Santa Barbara	Tide pools, Surfing, Kelp Beds for fishing. Lots of sea life visible.	Dog-friendly beach.

Beach	Location	Features	Comments
Leadbetter Beach	Shoreline Drive and Loma Alta, Santa Barbara	Scenic beach with lots of water sport activity. Great BBQ and picnic facilities.	Adjacent Shoreline Grill offers great grub right on the sand if you like. Bring your bikes and ride along the bike path.
West Beach	West Cabrillo Boulevard, Santa Barbara	Small, protected inlet good for tots. Playground nearby.	Yards away from West Beach wading pool and Los Banos Pool. Bring your bikes and ride along the bike path.
East Beach	East Cabrillo Boulevard, Santa Barbara	Clean, expansive, white sand beach. Sand volleyball courts. Children's playground and swings. Food available at the casual East Beach Grill.	The Bathhouse sells beach supplies and rents volleyballs, boogie boards, and more. Hot showers, lockers, and weight room also available. Bring your bikes and ride the bike path.
Summerland State Beach	End of Evans Avenue, Summerland	Playground and volleyball nets on the bluff above the beach.	Dog-friendly Beach. Lengthy ramp down to the beach.

Beach	Location	Features	Comments
Santa Claus Beach	Off Santa Claus Lane, Carpinteria	Gentle waves – tide pools - trains passing provide extra excitement.	Adjacent Santa Claus Lane has food options.
Carpinteria Beach	End of Linden Avenue, Carpinteria.	Calm water with no riptides – very shallow water – long stretch of sand. Lots of shells for collecting.	Great choice as you can walk into downtown Carpinteria for snacks, lunch and shopping.

Tide Pools

T he best time to explore the tide pools is during the lowest tide, preferably at the beginning of the low tide, as well as right after a storm. Check the Santa Barbara News Press tide tables, or www.sb-outdoors.org for daily conditions. Typical sea life you might find includes hermit crabs, mussels, sea anemones, sea urchins, barnacles, limpets and sea stars. While exploring, remember to be mindful of the fragile ecosystem you have encountered.

Rules to observe while visiting tide pools:

• Do not remove, collect, or harm any rocks, animals, shells, plants, sand, seaweed, etc.

• With groups of young children, be aware of the tide's movements and wave sets. Always visit during low tides.

• Walk around large rocks rather than step on them: fragile algae and animals may be smashed.

• Touch the animals in the water, but do not pick them. Animals that are removed from the rocks have a hard time getting back to them.

- Leave everything as you found it (if you move a rock, put it back when you finish your observations).

- Help keep the reserve clean by carrying all your trash back with you and picking up trash left by others.

Top Pick
Shoreline Park

Arroyo Burro State Park (aka Hendrys Beach)

Look near the rocks at the edge of the water at low tide. For a short hike, walk northwest, along the beach, towards More Mesa where you will find more colorful tide pool areas.

Location: Near the intersection of Las Positas Road and Cliff Drive, you will find a large parking lot for the beach.

Devereux Point (aka Coal Oil Reserve Point) & Sands Beach

Devereux Point is also called Coal Oil Point because of the numerous natural oil seeps in the area. It is one of the few rocky intertidal areas that is not seasonally covered with sand. Because of this, it is one of the better tide pooling areas. The area has medium to small sized boulders and is termed a 'turnable rock' tide pool area. By looking under the boulders, certain species can be found that do not occur in areas with solid rock.

Location: Park at the corner of Camino Majorca & Del Playa Roads in Isla Vista, Goleta. Walk along the marked paths and

The Great Outdoors

down the bluffs to the first point you see towards the north, this is Devereaux Point. The beach beyond this point is Sands Beach. It can be a bit of a hike with kids. If you would like to park closer, call the Reserve Director at (805) 893-5092 for a West Campus permit and parking information.

El Capitan State Beach

El Capitan State Beach has a beautiful sandy beach with rocky tide pools.

Location: The beach is located off Highway 101 seventeen miles northwest of Santa Barbara. Exit Hwy 101 at El Capitan State Beach and turn towards the coast. There is parking inside the park for about $3 - $5 day use. Ask the ranger for more information about the tide pool areas. Park in the lower day use parking lot. Take a short walk along the coast towards the Southeast.

Carpinteria State Park

This area is filled with solid rocks and thus termed a 'solid shale' tide pool. Be sure to see the Visitors Center which features an indoor tide pool, hours vary seasonally.

Location: Exit on Casitas Pass Road, off Hwy 101, and follow the signs to Carpinteria State Beach. Parking will cost around $5-8. Ask the Rangers for more information on where to park. From Carpinteria Beach walk down the beach towards Tar Pits to the 5 foot plus tall rock formations, an area known as Jelly Bowl.

Hammonds Beach

At lower tides the entire beach, almost all the way to Hammond's Point, becomes one long tide pool.

Location: The San Ysidro exit off Hwy 101 becomes Eucalyptus Lane on the ocean side. Drive a half mile to the beach access point. There are 12 parking spaces next to the beach. Go down the steps to Miramar Beach and head Northwest during low tide, towards Hammonds. You can also access a trailhead to Hammonds Beach up by the parking area.

Shoreline Park

This is a popular and easily accessible location to view thriving tide pools.

Location: Park along Shoreline Drive at the top of the hill, above Leadbetter Beach. There is a parking lot between La Marina and Las Ondas Drives. Follow the narrow wooden stairs to the beach and tidal pool area (when the tide is low).

UCSB Lagoon & Goleta Point

Near the UCSB Lagoon, massive rock benches jut out into the ocean creating a sensational tide pool area. UCSB requests that the public minimize disturbance to the sensitive habitats in the Goleta Point area, so please tread lightly.

Location: From Highway 101 in Goleta, head south on Ward Memorial Drive (Route 217). Take the Goleta County Beach exit and park in the large lot provided. If you want to park closer, stay on the highway to the UCSB kiosk. Parking on the weekend is $2. Ask for more information from the kiosk if it is staffed. Passing the kiosk, take the very next left turn. Drive to near the end of the road until you see a parking lot on your right. Park here. Walk on the beach, towards Goleta Point, passing some low sandstone cliffs that separate the campus from the sea until you reach the UCSB Lagoon. There are some excellent, well studied, tide pools in this area.

Seaside Wilderness Park, Ventura

It is not easy to access, but here you will find rare cobblestone tide pools.

Location: Take the "State Beaches" exit from Hwy 101 and turn North on Harbor Blvd. Drive until you reach Figueroa Street. Turn left and then right. There will be a free parking lot at Surfer's Point and a paid lot for Seaside Park. Walk north along the shoreline through the Seaside Wilderness Park, just north of the Ventura River, and around the tide pools along the cobbled shore.

Anacapa Island, Channel Islands

The protected environment on the island allows many species of plants and animals to thrive here. From Frenchy's Cove, a short hike over a rocky knoll takes you to Anacapa's south shore and a rocky tide pool habitat.

Location: Near Frenchy's Cove on Anacapa Island. You must take a ferry to the islands (see the section on the Channel Islands for ferry shuttle information). Ask the Rangers for more information about the tide pool locations on the island.

Outdoor Adventures With Short Strolls

Top Pick
Coronado Butterfly Preserve

Alice Keck Park Memorial Garden

Both children and parents will delight in the 4.6-acre botanical collection of this garden featuring a low water-using demonstration garden, picnic areas and a gazebo overlooking a lily pond. There is a koi pond which also hosts turtles, bass and bluegill.The sensory garden with audio posts and interpretive Braille signs is a unique feature of this park. Come to this garden when you are looking for a leisurely stroll with the kids. This garden is near downtown and across from the enormous Kids World play structure in Alameda Park.

Directions: Located on the corner of Garden and Micheltorena Street. The address is 1500 Micheltorena Street, Santa Barbara.

Andre Clark Bird Refuge

This 42-acre saltwater lagoon and bird refuge is a brackish wetland providing a safe haven for a diverse bird population which includes ducks and geese. Kids enjoy watching these birds as they frolic on the lagoon. There is a paved path around the lagoon for riding bikes with the kids or simply strolling. Coordinate this visit with your ride down Cabrillo Boulevard or visit to the zoo. Enjoy Mexican fare at Café Del Sol located across the street from the refuge.

Directions: Exit Cabrillo Boulevard from 101 Hwy and head towards the ocean. You will see it almost immediately. The address is 1400 East Cabrillo Blvd, Santa Barbara.

Carpinteria Bluffs and Seal Sanctuary

This adventure offers panoramic views of the Santa Barbara Channel, Carpinteria Valley and Santa Ynez Mountains. This 52-acre parcel includes hiking and biking trails, as well as numerous picnic spots. The blufftop overlooks a California harbor seal rookery. Children enjoy watching the harbor seals play in the water and sunbathe on the rocks. During the birthing season from December through May, volunteers guard the area to protect the newborns from human disturbance and to educate onlookers about the federally protected seals. The rookery at the Bluffs is the only one accessible to the public on the Southern California coast. Call (805)684-5479 or visit www.carpinteriabluffs.org to find out more about the birthing season.

Directions: Exit on Bailard Avenue from Hwy 101 in Carpinteria. Drive south towards the ocean and park at the end of the road

Length: 2 miles round trip

Elevation gain: None

The path starts at the end of Bailard Road. Hike towards the ocean through the meadow. Near the ocean bluff, take the path on the row that parallels the eucalyptus trees. At the end of the grove, cross the railroad tracks to the left. Continue along the edge of the bluffs to a bamboo fence – this is the seal sanctuary overlook. Return along the same path.

Chumash Painted Cave State Historic Park

Dating back to the 1600s, the drawings on this sandstone cave are well-preserved examples of Native American art. This artwork drawn by the Chumash Native Americans is religious in nature, although it also depicts the coastal fisherman of the era. The location of the canyon is steep and the road is narrow so approach the area carefully.

Directions: Take Highway 154 out of Santa Barbara and turn right on Painted Caves Road. The cave is located on the left, about two miles up a steep, narrow road. The pullout at the site will only accommodate one or two vehicles. Trailers and RVs should not attempt the road. Call (805) 968-1033 or visit www.parks.ca.gov for more information.

Coronado Butterfly Preserve and Ellwood Main Monarch Grove

Celebrated as one of the largest Monarch butterfly over-wintering groves in California, this 9.3 acre preserve is ripe with butterflies during the peak season from December through February. Children delight in witnessing these beautiful butterflies by the thousands, free to roam in their natural habitat among the eucalyptus groves. Short trails and information posts guide you through this open space preserve to the Ellwood Main Monarch Grove, Ellwood Shores Coastal Bluffs, Santa Barbara Shores County Park, the Devereux Slough and to the beach. The stroll outlined below will take you around the preserve and coastal bluffs.

Directions: Exit Glen Annie Road/Storke Road off Hwy 101 in Goleta. Turn towards the ocean (left if coming from downtown Santa Barbara) onto Storke Road. Take a right onto Hollister Avenue. Turn left onto Coronado Drive. Park alongside the posted butterfly preserve sign on the right. See www.sblandtrust.org/coronado.html

Length: 1 mile round trip or less

Elevation Gain: 40 feet

Follow the trail up the path past the information center. The trail will descend into the eucalyptus groves into the butterfly habitat. Cross a footbridge and veer to the left at a T-junction. Go deeper into the grove and at the next junction, take the right fork into the Ellwood Main Monarch Grove. Go up the hill until you reach a large meadow. A network of trails weaves across the bluffs. At this point, you can turn back towards the preserve and follow this trail back to Coronado Drive or follow one of the trails around the bluffs then return.

The Great Outdoors

Douglas Family Preserve (Santa Barbara Coastal Bluffs)

This 70-acre open space area that sits above Arroyo Burro Beach (aka Hendry's Beach) in the Mesa preserves 2,200 feet of exceptional undeveloped ocean frontage. The modest trails are sprinkled with eucalyptus, oak and cypress trees and views of the Pacific Ocean abound. This area is especially popular with dog owners due to the off-leash privileges.

Directions: Exit Las Positas Road from Hwy 101 in Santa Barbara. Head south towards the ocean to the end. Take a right on Cliff Drive. Turn left into the Arroyo Burro Beach parking lot.

Length: 1.5mile loop

Elevation Gain: 150 feet

Walk out the parking lot eastward - back towards Las Positas Road on Cliff Drive. Catch a trailhead over the bridge on Cliff Drive into a grove of trees. The trail veers left and up the hill. At the top, continue south along the edge of the preserve. Upon reaching the ocean bluffs, hike west along the cliffs. At the Arroyo Burro Beach overlook the trail swings to the right and loops back to the top of the hill where you will follow the trail back down to Cliff Drive.

Los Carneros County Park and Lake

This natural, historical and cultural preserve is home to a 25-acre lake filled with birds. Effortless walking paths lead around the lake and park from the historic Victorian Stow House built in 1872, and the South Coast Railroad Museum. Both offer tours and exhibits. Park features include BBQ Grills, Benches and Picnic Tables, Hiking and Biking Trails, Bird Watching, and Equestrian Trails.

Directions: Exit Los Carneros Road from Hwy 101 north-bound, in Goleta. Turn right towards the mountains. The

Stow House and Railroad Museum parking lot will be on your right hand side.

Length: 1.5 mile loop

Elevation Gain: none

Follow the rail fence from the parking lot up past the Stow House. Follow the signs to Los Carneros Lake. At the junction take a right onto the paved road that overlooks the lake. Follow the path around the lake. As you walk northbound facing the Santa Ynez mountains you will eventually head left following the shoreline and crossing a bridge over the wetland. The trail will lead you back to the paved road near the trailhead and parking lot. Children enjoy touring the Railroad Depot and taking a short ride on the Goleta Short Line miniature train ride which operates year-round (see www.goletadepot.org).

Nojoqui Falls

Conveniently located, yet far from civilization, Nojoqui is a perfect spot for family outings. Nojoqui is a Chumash Indian word that has lost its meaning. It is correctly pronounced "Na-hoo-ee". The park features a playground with BBQ grills and a picnic area. A short walk (half mile round trip) takes you to a spectacular set of falls that drop nearly 100 feet over a sandstone wall. All ages will enjoy the walk. The setting is lush, green and mystical - it feels like a scene from Lord of the Rings.

Directions: Take the 101 north from Santa Barbara past Gaviota and turn right onto Old Coast Highway. There is a sign for Nojoqui County Park. Turn onto Alisal Road and then right into the county park. The park is under 2 miles from the freeway.

Length: Half-Mile, round trip

Elevation Gain: None

You will see a trail head when you park. Follow it. The falls are straight ahead.

Refugio to El Capitan State Beach

Choose this hike at lower tide in order to avoid climbing around a large rock at high tide. There are wonderful tide pools along the way where you can spot large pinkish Sea Stars as well as other sea life. Walk along some secluded beaches and rustic coastline. There are snack bars and restrooms at both ends of the hike in case you need some creature comforts.

Directions: Start at Refugio Beach. Free parking is more accessible. Travel about 30 miles northbound on Hwy 101. Take the Refugio Exit. Turn left and park under the freeway overpass. You can park inside the campground but it is not free.

Length: 4.5 miles

Elevation Gain: 500 feet

Begin this hike at the snack bar at the beach, or just to the left of it, to the left of the little lagoon. Head back in the direction of Santa Barbara, walking along the beach. If you do not hit low tide, then a few places will be tough to navigate without splashing through the surf or climbing rocks. At one point, you can even hop onto the bike path until you reach sandy shoreline again, then return to the beach. Don't miss the Sea Stars in the tide pools at the rocky points. Turnaround when you reach the El Capitan campground. Either return via the shoreline, or try the Aniso Trail, an ancient Chumash trade route, which is a paved hiking and biking trail along the sea cliffs and marine terraces connecting El Capitan State Beach to Refugio State Beach.

Salt Marsh (El Estuaro)

Recognized as one of the most important wetlands in Southern California, this salt marsh is a busy, healthy ecosystem filled with rare birds, fish, snails, sharks and plants. This 230-acre reserve is one of the last remaining coastal estuaries in California. This wetland is fed by Franklin Creek and Santa Monica Creek. Kids enjoy following the nature trails, viewing the full color interpretive signs, and exploring the many observation decks. This nature park is a place of education, discovery, calm and wonder. Docent lead tours of the nature park are available on Saturdays at 10am – meet at the park name sign on Ash Avenue. Call (805)684-8077

Directions: Exit on Linden Avenue from Hwy 101 in Carpinteria, and turn right. Follow Linden to Sandyland Road and turn right again. Park at the end of Sandyland Road near the nature trail sign on Ash Avenue.

Length: 1 mile round trip

Elevation Gain: None

Start at the nature trail sign and walk to the observation deck to the northwest. Follow the meandering path to the right, away from the boardwalk that leads to the ocean. At the northeast end of the park, bear to the left towards another overlook of the wetland. Continue on the path to a T-junction and follow the left fork a short distance to the final observation deck. Return along the same path.

Tar Pits Park

Once the site of a Chumash Indian village, this 8-acre bluff-top park is named for the natural tar that seeps up from beneath the soil. The petrified tar mounds along the beach are residuals once used by the Chumash Indians for caulking canoes, sealing cooking vessels and making tools. In addition to exploring the tar mounds families can meander on walking trails, view numerous birds and vegetation, and relish spectacular views. Benches are placed along the bluffs edges for your comfort. Onlookers often see seals and dolphins in these waters. There is also a thriving tide pool. This area serves as Carpinteria surfers' social hub – you might catch some good wave riding while visiting.

Directions: Exit on Linden Avenue from Hwy 101 in Carpinteria. Turn right and drive to 6th Street and take a left.

The Great Outdoors

Turn right on Palm Avenue and drive into the Carpinteria State Beach parking lot – a parking fee is required.

Length: 1.5 miles round trip

Elevation Gain: 50 feet

Follow the sandy beach southeast towards Ventura. You will pass Carpinteria Creek then a footpath will take you onto a bluff to the campground road. Follow any of the interconnecting paths that continue to cross the blufftop terrace. Children are enchanted with the groves of eucalyptus trees and Monterey pines along the way. You will see a stairway leading to the shoreline. As you near the oil pier the path will narrow. You can either turnaround here or cross the ravine and continue until you reach the Carpinteria Bluffs (covered on the following hike in this book).

Anacapa Island - Channel Islands National Park

The five islands and surrounding waters that comprise the Channel Islands National Park and the Channel Islands National Marine Sanctuary have not been geared to mass tourism and the associated experience is unspoiled beaches and secluded lagoons teeming with wildlife, and uniquely preserved plant and animal species. The islands are Anacapa, Santa Cruz, Santa Rosa, San Miguel, and Santa Barbara. Each island has its own character. Anacapa is the typical entry point as it is tiny and closest to mainland. Santa Cruz is the largest and most biologically diverse. Santa Rosa has the most open space and is the most historically interesting. San Miguel has the most wildlife and best hiking, but is the most restrictive. Tiny Santa Barbara Island is the most isolated.

The islands offer a variety of recreational opportunities, such as SCUBA diving, snorkeling, swimming, bird watching, kayaking, whale watching, and sailing. On some of the islands families may camp, hike, picnic, and explore tide pools, isolated beaches, and rugged canyons.

Depending on the season, the boat ride to the islands offers children the opportunity to encounter many types of marine life including several species of seals, sea lions, whales and dolphins, as well as pelagic fish, and sea birds. Most of these species are also visible from the islands' beaches. From late December through March, the Eastern Pacific Gray Whale migrates through these waters. In the spring and summer, blue and humpback whales are drawn to the nutrient rich waters of the season.

Anacapa Island is one of the shortest distances from the mainland – under 2 hours from Santa Barbara and 1 hour from Ventura. Ask for a Junior Ranger booklet at the visitor's center, boat concessionaire offices, or on the island from a park ranger. The program helps children discover and protect the wonders of the island.

Directions: Upon landing, near the visitor center, there is a 1.5 mile self guiding nature trail that explores East Anacapa Island Trail. Visitors climb a staircase to reach the island plateau. From the plateau, the trek is an easy stroll with great views of nearby islets and islands. The trail passes the ranger station and island museum within the first half mile. At the museum, visitors can get an interpretive brochure that describes the unique features of the island. On calm summer days families can swim in the landing cove. At West Anacapa's Frenchy Cove, there is a beach and a snorkeling area. This is a great place for a picnic. Nearby, on the islands south side, there is an area ripe with tide pools. Kayaking is also very popular on this island due to the rich kelp beds that surround the land. The islands offer no concession services or fresh water, so bring plenty of water and liquids for the

The Great Outdoors

whole family, sunscreen and hats, extra sweaters, and lunch & snacks.

Contact Info: Channel Islands National Park Visitors Center
1901 Spinnaker, Ventura
(805) 658-5730
www.nps.gov / chis /

Transportation to the Islands:

Truth Aquatics (boats and tours depart from Santa
Barbara Harbor)
301 West Cabrillo Blvd, Santa Barbara
(805)962-1127
www.truthaquatics.com

Island Packers Inc (boats and tours depart from Ventura and
Oxnard Harbors)
1691 Spinnaker Drive, Ventura
(805)642-1393
www.islandpackers.com

Hikes

**Top Pick
San Ysidro Canyon**

Listed below are a selection of hikes in the Santa Barbara area that are relatively short, as well as low in elevation gain. Also taken into consideration for the enjoyment of the entire family were scenery and sense of adventure. For an extensive list of hiking trails in Santa Barbara county, complete with maps, topos and directions to the trailhead, visit www.SantaBarbaraHikes.com

TIPS:

- Watch out for Poison Oak
- Always wear sunscreen
- Bring snacks and water no matter the length of the hike
- Bring a compass for longer and more remote hikes

SHORT HIKES FROM PARK PLAYGROUNDS
(See Park Playground section for more information)

Some of the playgrounds listed under the park section have short, easy hiking trails that depart from the park. The hikes are covered here.

Elings Park: Sierra Club Trail

The developed northern side and the undeveloped southside divide this 236-acre park. The nature trails on the south side of the park lead up to a hilltop with panoramic views from the Santa Ynez Mountains to the Santa Barbara harbor and Channel Islands.

Directions: Exit Las Positas Road from Hwy 101 in Santa Barbara. Head south towards the ocean on Los Positas to the Elings Park entrance on the left. Enter the park on Jerry Harwin Parkway to the signed trailhead on the right, across from the soccer fields.

Length: 1.3mile loop

Elevation Gain: 300 feet

Take the right fork at the trailhead up the switchbacks to the hilltop ridge. Follow the trail along the ridge to the east – left of the switchbacks. The trail will start its descent down another set of switchbacks to the left again. Your loop is completed when you reach your starting point.

Lookout Park to Summerland Beach

A charming park and playground, Lookout Park sports an ocean view from its' grassy flat along the ocean bluffs. This 4 acre treasure boasts both a forested trail and paved walkways down to its' sandy beaches. Hike a short distance up the coast and your children will find tide pools rich with sea creatures. Children take pleasure in discovering the coves and rocky points along the walk.

Directions: In Summerland, take Evans Avenue towards the beach, the parking lot is at the end of Evans Avenue.

Length: Short Stroll

Elevation: 50 feet

Go to the left of the parking lot close to the railroad tracks. The trail will be marked with a sign. Pass through an open gate and follow the path through the eucalyptus grove, cross over a wood bridge, and head to the beach. Veer right on the shoreline. During high tide you cannot continue past this beach. When you are done exploring this quaint beach, then walk up the paved walkway back to the parking lot. During low tide, the shoreline to the northwest eventually reaches Eucalyptus Lane and Hammonds Meadow Trail (covered in this section). Look for the tide pools that are visible along the way.

Rocky Nook Park

Try this short little hike if you are looking for the great outdoors, just minutes from downtown. Sometimes a 30 minute, round trip adventure is just enough for the kids, and parents alike.

Directions: The entrance to this park is on your right just past the historic Santa Barbara Mission on Mission Canyon Road. Park next to the Trailhead to Foothill Road.

Length: Less than 1 mile, round trip

Elevation Gain: None

Take the trailhead towards Foothill Road. After about 10 minutes, you will hit the Fire Station. This is your turnaround point.

Stevens Park

This oak shaded park at the bottom of San Roque Canyon is home to a nature trail that rambles among creek beds and forest groves. The flora is quite similar to many of the hiking trails located in the lower Santa Barbara foothills, but the hike is much more leisurely.

Directions: Exit Las Positas Road off Hwy 101 in Santa Barbara. Drive northeast towards the Santa Ynez Mountains - Las Positas becomes San Roque after crossing State Street. Turn left on Calle Fresno. Turn right onto Canon Drive, and right again into the posted park entrance.

Length: 1.8 miles round trip

Elevation Gain: 175 feet

Take the footpath at the upper end of the park, aside San Roque Creek. Cross under the large bridge, through a tree grove to a grassy meadow on the right. At the trail split, veer left following the creek, passing a sandstone formation on the right. Descend and cross the creek into the large boulder area. Follow the trail up the hill, crossing two ridges, and over a concrete spillway to a wide path. Veer right on the wide path, and follow it down over the creek and uphill to a T-junction with Jesusita Trail. This is your turnaround point.

The Great Outdoors

Toro Canyon Park

This 74 acre park is located in the foothills between Carpinteria and Summerland. In addition to a playground for the kids, there are shady picnic spots near the stream. Children are always delighted to find a gazebo at the top of the hiking loop. In addition, the panoramic 360 degree views of the coastline, mountains and orchards make the top of the mile loop feel like quite an accomplishment for the whole family.

Directions: From Hwy 101 Southbound, near Summerland, exit on North Padaro Lane. Drive to Via Real and turn right. Continue to Toro Canyon Road and turn left. After a mile, you will see the signed Toro Canyon Park turnoff – take a right. After another mile, turn left into the park. Drive to the trail sign at the upper end of the park and park to the right.

Length: 1 mile

Elevation Gain: 300 feet

Follow the trail past the trailhead sign and across the stream towards the sandstone formation. Take the wide uphill path to the right of the formation. At the trail split take the left fork around the small knoll until you reach the gazebo at the hilltop. After experiencing the views and hilltop, continue west an complete the loop. Take a left, back towards the trailhead.

Tuckers Grove: San Antonio Creek Trail

The San Antonio Creek flows alongside this trail past meadows and tree groves. The near level terrain make this a comfortable walk for most and a popular jogging trail for many. The bay laurel, oak and sycamore trees along the creek shade the trail and make it a very pleasant choice on a hot day.

Directions: Exit on Turnpike Road off Hwy 101 in Goleta. Drive north, away from the ocean, and cross Cathedral Oaks

Road. Drive directly into the park and turn right, parking in the farthest parking area.

Length: 3.4miles roundtrip

Elevation Gain: 200 feet

From the parking lot, hike past the upper picnic ground, crossing through the log fence opening on the left. Follow the trail up alongside San Antonio Creek. After a mile, cross the creek twice. The trail ascends a hill and to the left over a concrete dam. After the dam, follow the trail to the right and cross back over the creek. Continue along the trail, next to a chainlink fence. The trail intersects with Hwy 154, under a large bridge. This is your turnaround spot.

BEACHSIDE HIKES

Goleta Beach and UCSB Lagoon

Explore the coastal bluffs that adorn the UCSB campus on this excursion to the UCSB lagoon. The tide pools at Goleta Point are a guaranteed attraction for the kids. On Saturdays you can also visit the Research Experience and Education Facility — the REEF, in the marine laboratory section of the hike. See more about the REEF under the Educational Exploration section.

Directions: Exit Ward Memorial Boulevard/Hwy 217 off Hwy 101 in Goleta. Continue to the Sandspit Road Exit and turn left at the stop sign. Drive to the beach parking lot turnoff, turning right and crossing the lagoon into the lot.

Length: 4 miles round trip

Elevation Gain: 50 feet

Hike along the park lawn northwest to the ocean bluffs. Continue beyond the natural bridge and walk parallel to the shoreline onto the UCSB campus. When you reach the marine laboratory take the right fork and cross the road towards the UCSB Lagoon.

Follow the path to the right of the lagoon making a loop around the lagoon. Upon return to the ocean, climb up to the bluff on the left and continue around the lagoon, descending the steps between lagoon and ocean. Cross the marine laboratory and return on the same path back to Goleta Beach.

Hammond Meadow Trail

This colorful, discrete trail lets visitors get a taste of the coastal lifestyle in Montecito. The trail roams through blossoming bougainvilleas and tall palm and eucalyptus trees...flora very routinely grown in Santa Barbara. Stroll among picturesque homes and alongside three beautiful beaches: Miramar, Hammonds, and Butterfly beaches.

Directions: From Hwy 101 southbound, exit onto San Ysidro Road in Montecito. Turn right towards the ocean onto Eucalyptus Lane and drive to a small parking lot at the end of the road. If it is full, park on a nearby road.

Length: Under 2 miles round trip

Elevation Gain: None

Follow the signed trail near the parking area, to the west, on through the colorful lane. Cross a bridge over Montecito Creek and continue creekside towards the ocean. Follow the shoreline. You will pass the Biltmore Hotel when you reach Butterfly Beach. Continue to the end of Butterfly Beach. This is your turnaround spot.

Lookout Park

(see Short Hikes from Park Playground Section)

Loon Point

Groves of sycamores, coastal oaks, Monterey cypress, and eucalyptus line the Toro Canyon Creek whose mouth empties into Loon Point. Along the adjacent isolated stretch of coastline and 40-foot cliffs is a path that leads to this point.

Directions: From Hwy 101 Southbound, exit on Padaro Lane south, near Summerland. Turn right towards the signed Loon Point Beach parking lot on the left.

Length: 3 miles round trip

Elevation Gain: none

Follow the Loon Beach access trail parallel to the railroad tracks. Bear to the left under the bridge and past the eucalyptus trees. Stay on the path which descends narrowly between the cliffs to the shoreline. Veer to the right on the beach along the bottom of the cliffside. Follow the shoreline towards Loon Point that can be seen protruding out towards the sea. In the event of high tide Loon Point may be inaccessible, however, during low tide, the hike can be extended past the point. Turnaround and return along the same path.

More Mesa

A 360-degree panoramic view of the Santa Ynez mountains to the Channel Islands, this ocean bluff trail in Goleta is an adventure for the whole family. If you are looking to take a short hike, then enjoy your day at the beach, this may not be your ideal choice as the secluded beach below the 120-foot bluffs is clothing-optional.

Directions: Exit Turnpike Road off Hwy 101 northbound in Goleta. Turn towards the ocean to Hollister Avenue and turn left. At Puente Drive, turn right – Puente Drive will become Mockingbird Lane. Park on Mockingbird Lane, near the Vieja Drive Intersection.

Length: 2.6 miles round trip

Elevation Gain: None

The trail begins at the end of the road past the metal gate. Cross the wide meadow towards the ocean. At half a mile the trail will hit the ocean bluff top lined with a eucalyptus grove. Take a right at the fork and follow the bluff top trail alongside the shoreline. You will hit a fence near homes. This is your turnaround spot.

INLAND HIKES

Cold Springs Canyon: East Fork to Montecito Overlook

Cold Spring Creek meanders through an alder, bay and oak forest. The steep canyon walls filled with creeks, deep pools, and waterfalls enthrall children. The highlight of the journey is the Montecito Overlook that offers an extensive vista of the Santa Ynez Mountains, Pacific Ocean, and Channel Islands.

Directions: Exit Hwy 101 Southbound at Hot Springs Road in Montecito. Turn Left to reach Hot Springs Road. Turn left onto Hot Springs Road and drive 2 miles up to East Mountain Drive and turn left. Drive another mile to the Cold Spring Trailhead on the right side of the road. Park along the road and make sure to lock your doors and remove or hide your valuables in the car.

Length: 3.2 miles

Elevation Gain: 900 feet

Follow the Cold Spring trailhead on either side of the creek as they will merge. After a short distance, you will pass a bench, pool and West Fork Trail. Follow the same trail where you will cross a creek and continue uphill past waterfalls and pools. Cross another creek and head up the switchbacks. After a mile, the trail will become a utility road. After a short distance, this road will lead you on the right hand side and up a knoll to Montecito Overlook. Turnaround and return the same route.

Inspiration Point at Mission Canyon

A popular hike during sunset, 1,750-foot Inspiration Point is named for its' stunning view of the city, Pacific Ocean and Channel Islands. Mission Canyon is home to sandstone formations, numerous waterfalls, and water carved pools.

Directions: From the Santa Barbara Mission (Los Olivos and Laguna Street), Head up Los Olivos toward the mountains. The road makes a jag and becomes Mission Canyon Rd. At the stop sign, turn right on Foothill Rd. At the stop sign and fire station, turn left onto Mission Canyon Rd. At the fork in the road, veer left on Tunnel Rd. Drive to the end of Tunnel Rd. and park. Walk to the end of the road, next to the large water tank and metal gate. This is the trailhead. (Be careful to park with your tires completely within the street line or you will be towed – always lock your doors and hide your valuables).

Length: 3.5 miles round trip

Elevation gain: 900 feet

Pass the trailhead gate along the curving road and over the bridge past Mission Creek. The paved road ends just under one mile at a junction. Take the left fork named the Jesusita Trail. Descend into the canyon and cross the creek. Follow the switchbacks up the canyon wall past the sandstone formations. There is a T-junction at the summit where you will take a left to follow the power access road until you see a footpath on the right leading into the bushes. This 300 yard path leads to the top of the boulders known as Inspiration Point. This is your turnaround spot. Be sure to keep an eye out for mountain bikers coming down the dirt access road.

Knapps Castle

Located atop the Santa Ynez Mountains, this stone relic sits on a rocky lookout point with unobstructed views of Santa

Ynez River Valley and beyond. Children hike in anticipation of finding this "castle" and its' many remains, including rock arches and stairways, fireplaces, and chimneys all set atop the lingering foundation. You can create your own story about a fantasy castle or share the true story of this private sandstone mansion built in 1916 and devoured by the Paradise Canyon Fire in 1940.

Directions: Take the State Street/Hwy 154 Exit off Hwy 101 in Santa Barbara. Head up Hwy 154 (San Marcos Pass) towards the mountains and drive about 8 miles to East Camino Cielo Road on the right. Take a right and continue another 3 miles. When you see a forest service gate on the left, continue another mile past Painted Cave Road and park at the pullouts on the right.

Length: Just under 1 mile

Elevation Gain: 100 feet

(Note: this "castle" sits on private property on which access is currently allowed).

Cross East Camino Cielo towards Santa Ynez Valley and hike past the Forest Service private property gate. The unpaved trail crosses the hill to a junction. Veer to the right past another "private property" gate. The castle will soon come into view on a lookout point in the distance. After you reach the castle and explore the ruins, turn around and hike back the same route.

Parma Park

Nestled in the foothills of Sycamore Canyon, this 200 acre park is very rustic which makes it a popular place with hikers, bikers, and dog walkers. Here you will find several seasonal creeks and canyons lined with live oaks and sage trees. The peaceful setting overlooks the surrounding hills and the trails are unmarked.

Directions: From the 101 Hwy in Santa Barbara take the Mission St. exit and drive towards the mountains. At the end turn left onto Laguna and then turn right onto Los Olivos. At the fork in the road bear left and drive until you reach the end. Turn right and follow Foothill Road (Route 192) until you see Parma Park. Park across the road if the gate is locked.

Length: 2.5 miles roundtrip

Elevation Gain: 300 feet

Hike past the entrance and over an old stone bridge to the picnic area. Follow the unmarked Rowe Trail to the right that leads downhill and over Sycamore Creek. Continue onto the ridge that heads parallel above Stanwood Drive. Farther along veer to the left onto the Parma Fire Road located on a scenic knoll. Here you will see Sycamore Canyon, Santa Ynez Mountains, and the Pacific Ocean. Continue towards the left, descending along the fire trail. Cross the Sycamore Creek and return to your starting point.

Rattlesnake Canyon

This is one of Santa Barbara's most popular hikes. The children will enjoy this enchanting canyon filled with flourishing fauna, dipping pools, a rock grotto, splashing waterfalls and stream crossings. Outlooks include a sweeping panorama of the Pacific Ocean and Channel Islands. Rest assured the trail was not named for any type of snake habitat, but for its winding canyon.

Directions: From the 101 Hwy in Santa Barbara, take the Mission St. exit and drive towards the mountains. At the end, turn left onto Laguna and then turn right onto Los Olivos. At the fork in the road bear left and drive until you reach the end. Turn right and follow Foothill Road (Route 192) to Mission Canyon Road and turn left. At Las Canoas Road turn right and follow the Skofield Park sign until you reach the trailhead about a mile up the road. Park in the pullouts near the stone bridge over Rattlesnake Creek or in Skofield Park.

Length: 3.5 miles

Elevation Gain: 1000 feet

Hike past the trail sign along the side of the stone bridge. Cross the creek to a wide trail and head left for another half mile until you reach a trail split. Continue along the narrower trail that descends into the creek. Cross the flowing creek and follow the switchback trail out of the canyon. Another mile along you will cross the creek again twice then the trail will climb to a large grassy meadow called Tin Can Flat. Turn around and return at the junction just beyond the meadow with Rattlesnake Canyon and Tunnel Connector.

San Ysidro Canyon

This trail leads up through the San Ysidro Canyon, along the San Ysidro Creek. Your children will be thrilled to encounter the small waterfalls, cascades and pools that decorate the upper canyon. The grand finale is a beautiful 60-foot waterfall named the San Ysidro Falls.

Directions: From Santa Barbara exit on San Ysidro Road off Hwy 101 in Montecito. Drive up to East Valley Road and turn right. Drive to Park Lane and turn left. Drive up to East Mountain Drive and veer to the left. The trailhead is on the right side along East Mountain Drive.

Length: 3.7 miles round trip

Elevation Gain: 1200 feet

Follow the trailhead sign on the right, parallel to a wooden fence. Continue along a tree covered lane past homes to a paved road. Go along the paved road to a dirt road. The dirt road will take you into the San Ysidro Canyon. Pass the Old Pueblo and McMenemy trail junctions. Follow the fire road past a gate and eroded sandstone wall. Past the wall you will see power lines crossing the trail, take the footpath on the right hand side, leaving the fire road. Travel up the canyon past the many cascades and pools passing many side paths. At 1.5 miles the steep ascent begins passing through a switchback and metal rails. Cross the stream, to the right is an offshoot trail to several pools, falls and cascades. Continue along the main trail to a fork which leads to the base of San Ysidro Falls on the right. This is the turnaround.

Lessons & Rentals

Top Pick
Wheel Fun Rentals

WHEELS

 Wheel Fun Rentals

Just about any wheeled transportation can be rented here. Choose from electric cars, mopeds, scooters, mountain bikes, beach cruisers, tandems or 4-wheel surreys that seat up to nine adults and two children. Rollerblades are also available for rent.

Contact Info: 101 State Street, Santa Barbara
(805) 966-2282
www.wheelfunrentals.com

SB Baby Company Jogger, Stroller, and Beach Gear Rental

Travel with the luxury of minimized baggage, without having to give up your active lifestyle… rent your gear. In addition to

The Great Outdoors

gear such as joggers, strollers, cribs, beds, and high chairs, they rent beach packages complete with a red wagon for two, and a kids cabana for added protection from the sun. Free delivery too!

Contact Info: (805) 275-2414, toll-free (877) 240-1360
www.SBbabyCo.com

HORSES

Horseback Riding at Circle Bar B

Trails wind through the woods to the mountains, crossing streams and passing waterfalls along the way. Guests enjoy views of the canyons, Pacific Ocean, and the Channel Islands.

Contact Info: 1800 Refugio Road, Goleta
(805)968-3901
www.circlebarb.com

Rancho Oso Horseback Riding

Riders for the guided trail rides must be at least 8 years old. Hand-lead rides for children 7 and under are also available. All riders receive personalized attention and instruction from the friendly Wranglers.

Contact Info: 3750 Paradise Road, Santa Barbara
(805)683-5110
www.rancho-oso.com

SURF

The Beach House

This beach store rents surfboards and wetsuits, and offers classes via Santa Barbara Surf Adventures.

Contact Info: 10 State Street, Santa Barbara
(805) 963-1281
www.surfnwear.com
www.santabarbarasurfadventures.com

Surf Happens

Both parents and children alike will enjoy the surf lessons, surf camps and outings designed specifically for the family. Their youth day camps are popular and start at age 5 and up. Parents can also indulge in private or group lessons tailored specifically for them. Surf Happens sponsors local surfing events in the area. Come home with a Surf Happens shirt and cap just to prove you did it!

Contact Info: 1117 Las Olas Avenue, Santa Barbara
(805)966-3613
www.surfhappens.com

A-Frame Surf Shop

This popular store is well known in the community and adjacent to some beginner waves. You can rent surfboards and wetsuits here and lessons are offered as well. The service and staff are very knowledgeable and friendly.

Contact Info: 3785 Santa Claus Lane, Carpinteria
(805) 684-8803
www.aframesurfshop.com

Santa Barbara Seals Surf School

Lessons and camps tailored for kids.

Contact Info: (805) 957-1070
www.santabarbaraseals.com

Santa Barbara Surf School

Their slogan: Learn to Surf – Guaranteed.

Contact Info: (805) 745-8877
www.santabarbarasurfschool.com

Surf Country

This store offers surfboard, bodyboard, and wetsuit rentals on a daily basis. In addition, they provide private surf lessons for all levels.

Contact Info: 5668 Calle Real, Goleta
(805) 683-4450
www.surfcountry.net

BOATS, KAYAKS, SCUBA & FISHING

Anacapa Scuba Diving Lessons, Rentals, and Trips

An extensive array of scuba rentals, as well as masks and snorkels are available here. Scuba boat trips are available here as well. Minimum age for participation is 10 years.

Contact Info: 22 Anacapa Street, Santa Barbara
(805) 963-8917
www.anacapadivecenter.com

Cachuma Lake Boat Rentals

Choose from Boats with or without motors, paddle boats, water bikes, or a leisurely patio deck boat with a large awning. All rentals include a clean boat, oars or paddle, anchor and rope, gasoline for rental motors and mandatory life jackets.

Contact Info: Highway 154, Santa Barbara
(805) 688-4040
www.sbparks.org/docs/cachumaboatrates.html

Paddle Sports of Santa Barbara

A full-service Kayak, Canoe, Outrigger & Water Sports center, here you can rent your own kayak and accessories, take a lesson, or join on one of the many guided coastal excursions.

Contact Info: 117B Harbor Way, Santa Barbara
(805) 899-4925, (888) 254-2094
www.kayaksb.com

Sailing Center Boat, Sail & Kayak Lessons, Rentals and Charters

Rent or charter virtually any vessel you desire – kayaks, sailboats, motorboats and yachts. The Santa Barbara Sailing Center is one of the largest accredited American Sailing Association (ASA) schools on the West Coast. The Sailing Center offers year round Youth Sailing and Kayaking guidance. Suggested age is 8 years and up.

Contact Info: 133 Harbor Way, Santa Barbara
(800) 350-9090
www.sbsail.com

SEA Landing

SEA Landing is located in the Santa Barbara Harbor and is a one stop access point to most things ocean... Boat Trips and Rentals, Fishing, Whale Watching, Jet Ski Rentals, Kayak Rentals, Scuba Diving, Channel Island excursions, etc. It also serves as a tackle shop and dive shop. Ask about their Fish Camp training offered on how to tie a hook, coast, use tackle and read marine conditions aboard the 65' Stardust.

Contact Info: Santa Barbara Harbor
(805)963-3564
www.sealanding.net

Santa Barbara Jet Boats and Jet Skis
Hourly rentals of late model 2 –4 person Sea Doo watercraft and jet boats, Waverunners, and Kawasaki Jet Skis, and state of the art pedal boats.

Contact Info: 301 W. Cabrillo Blvd., Santa Barbara
(805) 570-2351
www.sbjetboats.com

Angels Bait and Tackle - Fishing off the Pier

Rent fishing poles and tackle to fish along the pier (no license required) or ask about fishing trips aboard the Stardust. Children under 12 are welcome and half-day trips are available.

Contact Info: Stearns Wharf - Cabrillo Blvd, Santa Barbara
(805)965-1333

Tours

. . . .

> **Top Pick**
> **Land Shark**
> **Land and Sea Tours**
>
>

DOWNTOWN SANTA BARBARA AND BEYOND

Santa Barbara Trolley Company

Ride a trolley around Santa Barbara and enjoy the fully-narrated tours packed with anecdotes, and well-researched historical information that will delight and entertain guests of many ages. All the stops in Santa Barbara are convenient to shopping, dining and attractions. Your ticket is good for free re-boarding all day, which is great when you have kids with you. Trolleys operate daily every hour.

Contact Info: (805) 965-0353
www.sbtrolley.com

Santa Barbara's Red Tile Walking Tour

Stop into the Visitors Center on Garden Street and Cabrillo Avenue to pick up a Red Tile Map. This self-guided tour highlights about twenty five selected sites covering about twelve blocks. While the map is not tailored towards kids specifically, you can choose your tour sites based on your needs.

Contact Info: 1 Garden Street, Santa Barbara
(805) 965-3021
www.sbchamber.org

Lotusland Garden Family Tours

Come marvel at this unique 37-acre estate and unrivaled botanic garden created by Madame Ganna Walska. Family tours for all ages are offered the first Thursday morning of each month, and the third Thursday afternoon of each month. Family tours are child and parent friendly and are separate from regular adult tours. Open February through November.

Contact Info: (805) 969-9990
www.Lotusland.org

OUTDOOR WILDERNESS AND ADVENTURE

Santa Barbara Adventure Company

Offering just about any adventure you could wish for in Santa Barbara. Choose from hiking, mountain biking, coastal kayak-

The Great Outdoors

ing, surf lessons, wine tours by van or bike, rock climbing, and sunset cruises. There are so many choices that you will have to visit their web site for all the details.

Contact Info: (805) 898-0671, (888) 773-3239
www.sbadventureco.com

Cloud Climbers Jeep & Wine Tours

Jump into a jeep and buckle up. Discover the mountains and backcountry of beautiful Santa Barbara! The Family Discovery Tour takes you from the coast, up the San Marcos Pass and across the ridge of the rugged Santa Ynez Mountains. Along the way your driver/guide will challenge you with a special, "Discovery Game". Children must be age 6 or over – bring your own booster seat.

Contact Info: (805) 965-6654
www.ccjeeps.com

Cachuma Lake Wildlife & Eagle Cruises

Climb aboard the 45-passenger "Osprey" for a 2-hour lake tour with a naturalist. From November through February, tours focus on the Bald Eagles and unusual birds who make Cachuma Lake their winter home. From March through October, the cruise takes a look at area wildlife, wildflowers, and resident birds along the shore. Appropriate for all ages.

Contact Info: Cachuma Lake (805) 686-5050 weekdays,
(805) 686-5055 weekends
www.sbparks.org/DOCS/lakecruise.html

SANTA BARBARA HARBOR

 Land Shark Land and Sea Tours

Try an excursion by land and by sea! For a unique experience, try the Land Shark, an amphibious tour vehicle hosting a personally narrated 90-minute land and sea adventure. Kids can see the historic Mission, Sea Lions, and find sunken treasure all from the same seat. There is no age limit.

Contact Info: (805) 683-7600
www.out2seesb.com

Capt. Don's Pirate Cruises

All aboard the Harbor Queen for a Pirate Tour. Tours depart every half hour during high season, from Stearns Wharf. Sail to Sea Lion Buoy or around the harbor. Enjoy Whale Watching cruises. Perfect for the kids!

Contact Info: Stearns Wharf, Santa Barbara
(805) 969-5217
www.captdon.com

WHALE WATCHING

Santa Barbara Sailing Center Tours

Choose from whale watching expeditions, Channel Island getaways and sailing for families. There are a great number of boats to choose from. Call for information.

Contact Info: 133 Harbor Way, Santa Barbara
(805) 962-2826
www.sbsail.com

Condor Cruises

Select from whale watching, channel island excursions, sport-fishing, and more. The Condor Express vessel features a modified hydrofoil "wing" mounted between the hulls which provides lift to raise the boat at high speed and produce the smooth ride.

Contact Info: 301 W. Cabrillo Blvd., Santa Barbara
(805) 882-0088
www.condorcruises.com

The Great Outdoors

Sunset Kidd Sailing Cruises & Whale Watching

Children are exhilarated upon boarding a sailboat. Santa Barbara harbor boasts a plethora of sea life including sea lions, seals, dolphins and whales. Public cruises are offered on a daily basis aboard the Sunset Kidd.

Contact Info: 125 Harbor Way, Santa Barbara
(805) 962-8222
www.SunsetKidd.com

KAYAKING

Captain Jacks Santa Barbara Kayak and Hiking Tours

Explore the concealed beaches and isolated Gaviota coast by land and by sea. Tours include transportation, professional guides, kayak equipment, lunch, hikes, and lots of fun. No experience necessary.

Contact Info: (888) 810-8687
www.captainjackstours.com

Santa Barbara Kayak Tours

Choose from a variety of tours nearby the wharf and harbor. Also available are surf lessons as well as kayak, surfboard, and body board rentals.

Contact Info: (805) 708-2346
www.sbkayaks.com

Paddle Sports Guided Coastal Excursions

A full-service Kayak, Canoe, Outrigger & Water Sports center, here you can rent your own kayak and accessories, take a lesson, or join on one of the many guided coastal excursions.

Contact Info: 117B Harbor Way, Santa Barbara
(805) 899-4925, (888) 254-2094
www.kayaksb.com

Aquasports

This group specializes in kayaking tours covering from Santa Barbara to the Channel Islands, as well as up towards San Luis Obispo.

Contact Info: 111 Verona Avenue, Goleta
(805)968-7231
www.islandkayaking.com

Island Packers

Contact this outfit for transportation to and kayaking at the Channel Islands.

Contact Info: (805)642-1393
www.islandpackers.com

Truth Aquatics Channel Islands Excursions & Scuba Diving

Offering Scuba Diving Trips and Channel Island Excursions including kayaking, snorkeling, and hiking. Truth Aquatics is "an official concessionaire to the Channel Islands National Park" which grants them the rights to land passengers on the islands for hiking or camping on both single and multiple day excursions.

Contact Info: 301 W. Cabrillo Blvd., Santa Barbara
(805) 962-1127
www.truthaquatics.com

PRIVATE CHARTERS

Channel Cat Catamaran Charter

This Cat, an 85-foot, three level, 107-ton luxury, sailing, catamaran is the stuff of fantasy and one of the world's most ingeniously built yachts. It is available for charter.

Contact Info: 6 Harbor Way, Santa Barbara
(805) 898-1015
www.channelcatcharters.com

WaveWalker Fishing Charters

Reserve your own private adventure aboard the beautiful modern custom 6-pak charter boat.

Contact Info: 691 Camino Campana, Santa Barbara
(805) 964-2046
www.wavewalker.com

Camping & Cabins

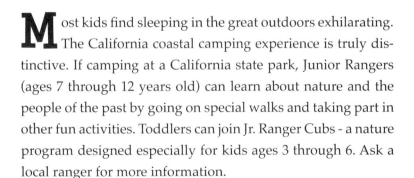

Top Pick
El Capitan Canyon

Most kids find sleeping in the great outdoors exhilarating. The California coastal camping experience is truly distinctive. If camping at a California state park, Junior Rangers (ages 7 through 12 years old) can learn about nature and the people of the past by going on special walks and taking part in other fun activities. Toddlers can join Jr. Ranger Cubs - a nature program designed especially for kids ages 3 through 6. Ask a local ranger for more information.

Cachuma Lake

This year round, full service Santa Barbara County Park offers Lake Cruises, Guided Nature Walks, a Nature Center, Boat

Rentals, Fishing, and Hiking. The scenic Cachuma Grill sits in the harbor and serves breakfast and lunch daily, and there is a well-stocked general store and gas station on site. The kids will be drawn to the Family Fun Center with swimming pools, miniature golf, bicycle rentals, video arcade and snack bar. If you are not interested in pitching a tent, try renting one of the lakeside yurts featuring platform beds to sleep 5 to 6, lockable door, inside lighting and heating, and screened windows. Campsites are first-come, first-serve which makes this site more promising during the peak summer season if you have made no previous reservations at state beaches. Be sure not to miss the nature center which hosts an impressive array of life-sized, local animal displays. Ask about the special program whereby kids 3 and up can become a Junior Ranger and learn about nature, wildlife, and the environment, and earn a cool patch!

Contact Info: HC 59 - Highway 154, Santa Barbara
(805) 686-5054
www.cachuma.com

Carpinteria State Beach

A charming campground located directly on the edge of the shoreline at beach level. It is a conveniently situated campground as the kids can play on the beach adjacent to your tent, or you can walk to downtown main street (Linden Avenue) which is one block away. Make sure to take the kids to the historic Robitailles candy shop on Linden Avenue – famous for their mints, this candy shop makes all the candy onsite.

Contact Info: (805) 968-1033
www.parks.ca.gov

Circle Bar B Guest Ranch and Cabins

Offering a variety of accommodations, this ranch makes sure that adults and kids alike won't run out of things. Choose from horseback riding, exploring, hiking, or take a refreshing dip in the pool or heated hot tub. Play a game of pool, foosball (table soccer) and table tennis in the game room. An added bonus is the Circle Bar B Theater whose dinner shows are usually warm, funny and engaging enough for preteens.

Contact Info: 1800 Refugio Rd, Goleta

(805)968-3901

www.circlebarb.com

(805)967-1962 - Dinner Theatre

www.circlebarbtheatre.com

El Capitan Canyon

Come experience "camping" at its' finest. The adventure is not about pitching tents in the dark, but enjoying the comfortable surroundings in your Cedar Cabin or Safari tent accommodations, among the oak and sycamore groves. Cabins are equipped with full bathrooms, linens, towels, kitchenettes, private picnic tables and fire pits. There is a well-equipped country store and café on the grounds for those who really want to travel lightly. The adjacent El Capitan Ranch offers horseback riding, and carriage rides, with scenic vistas. During the summer, the weekend concert series and popular BBQ dinner are especially enjoyable for the whole family.

Contact Info: 11560 Calle Real, Santa Barbara

(866) 352-2729

www.elcapitancanyon.com

El Capitan State Beach

Most of the campsites are nicely secluded at this coastal California State Beach Campground. The beach below the bluff-top campground is pristine and private. There are restrooms with showers, hiking trails and bike path trails. Bring the kids' trikes, bikes, or skateboards to enjoy along the wonderful bike trail that winds along the campgrounds. Try to choose a campsite farthest away from the freeway and railroad tracks. While the trains are a fun spectacle for the kids, it can be loud at midnight. Call ahead to make reservations if you are planning a visit during peak season in the summer.

Contact Info: (805) 968-1033
www.parks.ca.gov

Gaviota State Park

Soldiers of the Portola Expedition in 1769 termed this section of the coast as "gaviota" (seagull). This campground is popular for swimming, surf fishing and hiking. Divers and surfers make use of the pier on the west end of the beach.

Contact Info: (805) 968-1033
www.parks.ca.gov

Jalama Beach Park

Campers line up daily for the chance to stay at this first-come, first-serve beachside campground, only group campgrounds can be reserved in advance. The location is pristine with all campgrounds either beachside or ocean view. The facilities are ideal for families, with a wonderful play structure in the center of camp, basketball courts, and the famous Jalama Store and Grill. Just stepping into the store gives you a sense of the history of the location. Do not leave the campground without first trying the famous Jalama Beach Burger at the grill – it will leave you anticipating your next visit to the area.

The Great Outdoors

Contact Info: Recorded Information (805) 736-6316,
Park Office (805) 736-3504
www.sbparks.org
www.jalamabeach.com

Lake Casitas Recreation Area

Twelve campgrounds are scattered throughout the park – some are lakeside, some hillside, and some nestled among the trees. Choose from remote or centrally located. While swimming in the lake is prohibited, there is a fantastic water park for children under 12 on the premises.

Contact Info: 11311 Santa Ana Road, Ventura
(805) 649-2233, (805) 649-1122 Reservations
www.lakecasitas.info

Ocean Mesa at El Capitan

Surrounded by Los Padres National Forest above and the magnificent Pacific Ocean below, this campground also offers the best of modern camping life including an up-to-date heated pool and spa, laundry facilities, Internet, ATM and convenience store. Campers can enjoy a music-filled Saturday evening under the stars at El Capitan Canyon during the summer months.

Contact Info: (866)410-5783
www.oceanmesa.com

Rancho Oso Guest Ranch and Stables

Step back in time and add a taste of western flavor to your California camping experience. Rancho Oso has all of the classic resort amenities (pool, spa, tennis court, store, meals, activities, etc) to make your family vacation more appealing. Either bring your tent or camper, or choose to sleep in their old west cabins or covered wagons. To round out the wild, wild west extravaganza, horse riding and lessons are available and popular, and the riding trails are picturesque and plentiful.

Contact Info: 3750 Paradise Road, Santa Barbara
(805) 683-5686
www.rancho-oso.com

Refugio State Beach

Refugio State Beach offers first-rate coastal fishing, as well as hiking trails and picnic sites. For those seeking a 'southern California' landscape, palm trees planted near Refugio Creek adorn the beach and camping area. The bike trail along the beach bluff connects the beach with El Capitán State Beach.

Contact Info: (805) 968-1033
www.parks.ca.gov

Channel Islands National Park

The pastoral and unharmed nature of the islands makes camping here a distinctive experience. Camping is allowed on all five islands and conditions are primitive. All campgrounds are equipped with pit toilets and picnic tables, but no trash service is provided so campers must pack out their trash. For a family camping trip, Anacapa and Eastern Santa Cruz Island are the best choices. As opposed to the other islands, the campsites are only ½ mile from the landing and the boat ride from the mainland is shorter. Only Santa Cruz Island offers water so you must pack in water to Anacapa. Call the information line for more specifics about camping on the islands.

Contact Info: 1901 Spinnaker Drive, Ventura
(805) 658-5730, (805) 658-5711(Reservations)
www.nps.gov/chis/

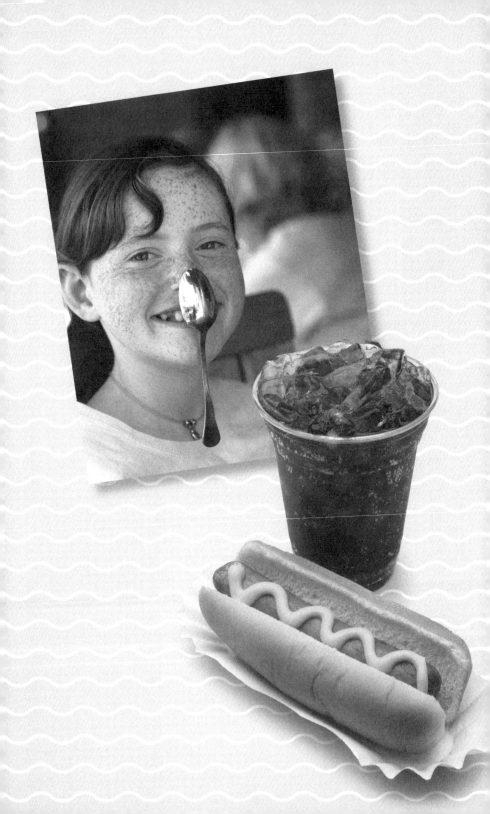

Kid Friendly Establishments

Please keep in mind that hours and locations are subject to change. Always call ahead to confirm.

Places To Eat

Many restaurants in Santa Barbara recognize the child visitor and have special menus, as well as crayons, coloring pages, and sippie cups to accommodate the little guest. The establishments listed in this section are selected primarily based on their kid-friendly menus and atmosphere.

SELF-SERVICE

Beach Grill at Padaro

Tables are placed along a half-acre lawn adjacent to the beach. Kids of all ages love the centrally located, giant sandbox chock full of sand toys. If you are lucky, a train will roll by and add to the kid's entertainment. The food is delicious and the service is excellent. While there is indoor seating, the grill is best known for its relaxed outdoor atmosphere, complete with wine and beer for mom and dad. Bring a light jacket in case the ocean breeze rolls through.

Hours: M-Thu 11 – 8, Fri 11-9, Sat 10-9, Sun 10-8

Contact Info: 3765 Santa Claus Lane, Carpinteria
(805) 566-3900
www.beachgrillpadaro.com

Char West

This is our favorite stop on the wharf for fish & chips, as well as corn dogs.

Hours: Mon-Thu 11-5, Fri-Sun 11-7

Contact Info: 221 Stearns Wharf, Santa Barbara
(805) 962-5631

East Beach Grill

Popular for its pancakes, this self-service eatery is located on the East Beach strand, and next to a play structure on the sand. Seating is primarily outdoors and the place is chock full of families. It is ultra casual dining - shoes are optional.

Hours: Weekdays 7am-4:30, Weekends 6am-5pm

Contact Info: 1118 E Cabrillo Blvd, Santa Barbara
(805) 965-8805

The Habit Burger Grill

A Santa Barbara classic, you'll be hard pressed to find a native in town who has not sampled the famous Habit charburger or albacore sandwich. You'll know when you are near The Habit because you cannot miss the smell of the charbroiled meat in the air. The kids menu is well-rounded and tasty.

Hours: M-Sat 10:30-9, Sun 11-8

Contact Info: 216 S. Milpas, Santa Barbara – (805) 962-7472
628 State Street, Santa Barbara – (805)892-5400
5735 Hollister, Goleta – (805)964-0366
www.habitburger.com

Los Gallos

There is plenty of debate over the best taqueria in town, and this establishment is one of the top contenders. The food is delicious and the salsa bar is excellent. The kids love the colorful chairs and the kids menu is an added bonus.

Hours: Daily 11am-9pm

Contact Info: 2009 De La Vina Street, Santa Barbara
(805) 563-4883

Luigi's Pizza and Pasta

There is pizza, and there is pasta, but most importantly, there are games! This is Santa Barbara's version of Chuck E. Cheese entertainment. Kids use tokens to play a variety of games in a designated arcade room and win prizes with their earned tickets.

Hours: Sun-Thu 11am-10pm, Fri-Sat 11am-11pm

Contact Info: 5711 Calle Real, Goleta
(805) 964-6433

The Natural Café

For those seeking the "granola" cuisine that California is typically associated with, you'll need to look no further. The food is delicious and the kids menu is a nice change from the typical.

Hours: Daily 11-9

Contact Info: 508 State Street, Santa Barbara – (805)962-9494
361 Hitchcock Way, Santa Barbara – (805)563-1163
5892 Hollister Ave, Goleta – (805)692-2363
www.thenaturalcafe.com

Nordstrom Café

While not a tourist attraction, this café in the Nordstrom department store top floor is a welcome stop if you are in the vicinity of the Paseo Nuevo Mall in downtown Santa Barbara. You'll find a full children's menu with complimentary Café cup souvenir, a family restroom and a mother's room nearby. The store can also check your packages.

Hours: 10 – 6

Contact Info: 17 W. Canon Perdido, Santa Barbara
(805) 564-8770
www.nordstrom.com

Reyes Market

If you are in Carpinteria looking for a genuine experience, look no further. The whole experience from food to atmosphere is authentic, and the service is always friendly. Most of the food items are a la carte and affordable so there is no need for a kids menu. If you are in need of a bribe, there are some Mexican toys and candies available in the small market.

Hours: Daily 8am-8pm

Contact Info: 4795 Carpinteria Avenue, Carpinteria
(805) 684-2212

Santa Barbara Chicken Ranch

Priding itself on authentic Mexican style mesquite Bar-b-Que, this informal eatery is genuine and popular at lunch. Kids can watch the orders prepared in full view from the open mesquite grill. Get a bucket of chicken to go!

Hours: Daily 11-10pm

Contact Info: 2618 De La Vina Street, Santa Barbara
(805) 569-1872
163 N Fairview Avenue, Goleta - (805)692-9200
www.sbchickenranch.com

Santa Barbara Shellfish Company

Grab a bench and have a shellfish feast on one of the outdoor picnic tables while taking in the sights of the pier – fishermen, seagulls, and boats. Be sure to bring a light coat in case there is a breeze.

Hours: Daily 11-9

Contact Info: 230 Stearns Wharf
(805) 966-6676
www.sbfishhouse.com

Super Cuca's Taqueria

For an animated experience, try Super Cuca on the Westside (there are 3 locations). The service is fast, the portions are huge, seating is an outdoor covered patio, and the kids menu includes burgers and fries. Bring plenty of quarters for the gumball and toy machines at the entrance.

Hours: Daily 6am-10pm

Contact Info: 626 W Micheltorena Street, Santa Barbara
(805) 962-4028

Woody's BBQ

Rustic in nature, Woody's serves up BBQ, games, televisions and an Old West theme making an adventure for kids and comfortable for parents. Kids can roam freely while mom and dad take a break. There is an old fashioned bathtub placed in the restaurant as a sink for washing hands – the kids always get a kick out of it.

Hours: Weekdays 11-9, Weekends 11am-11pm

Contact Info: 5112 Hollister Avenue, Goleta
(805) 967-3775
www.woodysbbq.com

Kid Friendly Establishments

Chuck E. Cheese

For a high dose of stimulation you will have to head on down to Ventura. This national chain is well known to most parents. Visit the web site before you go and print out valuable coupons for your visit.

Hours: Sun-Thu 9am-10pm, Fri & Sat 9am-11pm

Contact Info: 4714 Telephone Rd., Ventura
(805) 644-9777
www.chuckecheese.com

INFORMAL SIT DOWN

Breakwater Restaurant

You can't beat this location if you are looking for some harbor atmosphere. Well regarded for its popular breakfast, this casual café serves up a satisfying dinner also. The kid's menu is served for lunch and dinner only.

Hours: Sun-Thu 7am-8pm, Fri-Sat 7am-9pm

Contact Info: 107 Harbor Way, Santa Barbara
(805) 965-1557

California Pizza Kitchen

Home of the Original BBQ Chicken Pizza. The menu is not limited to just pizza, there is a hearty selection of pasta, salads, and desserts. While this restaurant is nothing unique to Santa Barbara, its' menu and atmosphere make it welcoming for families… right down to the crayons and activity books for the kids.

Hours: Sun-Thu 11-10, Fri & Sat 11 -11

Contact Info: 719 Paseo Nuevo, Santa Barbara
(805) 962-4648
www.cpk.com

Elephant Bar and Restaurant

This is the best place to take your kids if they like to watch airplanes take-off and land. The location is adjacent to the local airport. Choose a table in the back of the restaurant facing the airport. No need to worry about your noise levels as the atmosphere is especially lively here.

Hours: Sun-Thu 11am-10pm, Fri-Sat 11am-11pm

Contact Info: 521 Firestone Rd, Goleta
(805) 964-0779
www.elephantbar.com

Endless Summer

If you find yourself strolling around the Harbor in search of a kids menu and friendly service, go ahead and take a seat here. Many tables include a beautiful view of the harbor as well.

Hours: Mon-Thu 11:30-2:30 & 4-9, Fri-Sun 11:30-10pm

Contact Info: 113 Harbor Way, Santa Barbara
(805) 564-4666
www.endlesssummerbarcafe.net

Enterprise Fish Company

The Enterprise Fish Company, located near the waterfront in Santa Barbara, is a lively and family friendly restaurant. Portions are large and there is a complete children's menu.

Hours: Sun-Thu 11:30-10, Fri & Sat 11:30-11pm

Contact Info: 225 State Street, Santa Barbara
(805) 962.3313
www.enterprisefishco.com

Esau's Café

This family-owned, retro diner is located in downtown Carpinteria, very close to the beach and train station. The bright orange booths, friendly atmosphere, and delicious food make it a satisfying choice for parents. The crayons and kid menu are the icing on the cake. Take the train down to Carpinteria for breakfast and a beach visit, all within a block of each other.

Hours: Daily 7am-2pm

Contact Info: 507 Linden Avenue, Carpinteria - (805) 684-1070

IHOP (International House of Pancakes)

Yes, this is the restaurant chain that spans the entire nation. This casual diner caters to kids with creative food presentations, and indestructible environment. There is routinely a special offer on the menu celebrating the most current holiday or special event. Their slogan: Come hungry. Leave happy.

Hours: Daily 6am-10pm

Contact Info: 1701 State Street, Santa Barbara
(805) 898-1886
www.ihop.com

Longboards Grill

This quintessential surf-themed California restaurant is located on Stearn's Wharf. The upper-floor, open air patio location equips the establishment with a 360-degree coastal panorama. There are open barrels of roasted in the shell peanuts for the taking. There is always a special something for the kids like a treasure chest full of toys to choose from, on the house! Your active child will not be noticed in this lively atmosphere.

Hours: Daily 11:30am-11 pm

Contact Info: 210 Stearns Wharf, Santa Barbara
(805)963-3311

Marmalade Cafe

If your shopping excursion lands you in the La Cumbre Plaza, then step into this café for a nice variety of choices for breakfast, lunch or dinner. It originated as a catering company in Southern California and the menu is colorful and varied.

Hours: Mon - Fri 7:30am-10pm, Sat 8am-10pm,
Sun 8am-9:30pm

Contact Info: 3825 State Street, Santa Barbara
(805) 682-5246
www.marmaladecafe.com

Mesa Café

This home-style, local eatery is tough to spot from the road because it is in a shopping center. The décor is surf meets diner and the service is friendly, however, nothing beats their $2.50 Margarita for taking the edge off at the end of the day.

Hours: Daily 6am-10pm

Contact Info: 1972 Cliff Drive, Santa Barbara
(805) 966-5303

Ruby's Diner

This retro-Americana diner is also a national chain. It is centrally located in Santa Barbara at the Paseo Nuevo Mall, and a good choice when you are in the mall or strolling on nearby State Street. Very kid friendly in nature, the atmosphere is lively with many little distractions for the little guest. The kids' menu is abundant and the crayons are plentiful.

Hours: Sun-Thu 8am -9pm, Fri & Sat 8am-10pm

Contact Info: 601 Paseo Nuevo, Santa Barbara
(805) 564-1941
www.rubys.com

Beach Cafe

achside dining, and then there is dining directly
beach. Tables and chairs at this popular café are placed
directly on the sand. The view is magnificent and you will dine
with the luxury of having your kids occupied for an unlimited
time while they play on the beach. Bring some sand toys.

Hours: Weekdays 10am-Sunset, Weekends 8:30am-Sunset

Contact Info: 801 Shoreline Drive at Leadbetter Beach,
Santa Barbara
(805)568-0064

The Brewhouse

The menu is diverse, the portions are plentiful and the service
is friendly. The atmosphere is lively and your restless children
will not be noticed. Come on Sunday afternoon for specials on
the menu… the staff has been known to accommodate requests
with viewings of SpongeBob SquarePants, and the like, on the
large screen TVs.

Hours: Sun-Thu 11am-11pm, Fri & Sat 11am-12pm

Contact Info: 229 W Montecito St, Santa Barbara, 93101
(805) 884-4664
www.thebrewhousesb.com

Something's Fishy

The main entertainment at this Japanese Steakhouse & Sushi
Bar is the teppan grill tables and cooking showmanship that
is sure to delight the children. There is even a children's menu
for the teppan grill. If you would like to satisfy your craving
for sushi and need to satisfy the children as well, try this restaurant for dinner before 6pm on Monday through Thursday
when the sushi is half-priced.

Hours: Mon-Thu 11:30am-9pm, Fri-Sat 11:30am-10pm, Sun 11:30am-9pm

Contact Info: 500 State Street, Santa Barbara
(805)966-6607
www.somethingsfishyrestaurant.com

Summerland Beach Café

Home-style cooking and enormous portions keep families coming back to this local café. The kids' meals are equally gigantic. Established in an 1893 Victorian house, the setting includes ocean breezes, outdoor patios, and friendly service. Not open for dinner.

Hours: Mon-Fri 7am- 3pm, Sat & Sun 7am- 4pm

Contact Info: 2294 Lillie Avenue, Summerland
(805) 969-1019
www.summerlandbeachcafe.com

Taffy's Pizza

Most pizza parlors don't offer kids menus, but this one does… and it includes spaghetti! Tasty pizza, a patio on warm nights, a game room, televisions and plenty of space make this a terrific family choice, especially if you have a range of ages in your family. The fireplace can also make this place cozy on one of those rare cold days in town.

Hours: Mon-Thu 11am-9pm, Fri-Sat 11am-10pm, Sun Closed

Contact Info: 2026 De La Vina, Santa Barbara
(805) 687-3083
www.taffyspizza.com

UPSCALE

Chuck's Waterfront Grill

If you are looking for surf & turf menu options, then Chuck's may be your destination. Located directly on the harbor, the indoor décor is nautical in nature, and the kids menu is extensive and satisfying. The Maritime Museum is next door and worth a visit with the kids – see the Santa Barbara Historic Site Section.

Hours: Daily 5pm-10pm

Contact Info: 113 Harbor Way, Santa Barbara
(805) 564-1200
www.chuckswaterfrontgrill.com

Cold Spring Tavern

Drive 15 minutes into the Santa Ynez Mountains and go back 130 years in California history. This stagecoach way station has been serving up great food and drink since 1865. The historic tavern has been carefully preserved, as have the adjacent Road Gang House and Ojai Jail. The kids will get an authentic taste of the Wild, Wild West.

Hours: Mon-Sun 11am-2:45pm, 5pm-8:30pm, also Sat-Sun Breakfast 8am-11am

Contact Info: 5995 Stagecoach Road, Santa Barbara
(805) 967 0066
www.coldspringtavern.com

Los Arroyos Mexican Restaurant

A favorite among Montecito locals, this is not a traditional taqueria. The food and ambience redefine the notion of Mexican cuisine. The kids' portion is generous and scrumptious.

Hours: Mon-Fri 11am-9pm, Sat 9am-9pm, Sun 9am-8pm

Contact Info: 1280 Coast Village Road, Montecito
(805) 969-9059

Palace Grill

Best known for the delicious Cajun food and a lively atmosphere, this is a colorful and animated restaurant adjacent to downtown State Street. The noise level is perfect for a family visit. Come on a Tuesday night when beads are handed out, or Friday night for the magic show. The crayons and kids menu at lunch make afternoons a good option also.

Hours: Lunch Daily 11-3, Dinner Sun-Thu 5:30-11pm, Fri & Sat until midnight

Contact Info: 8 East Cota Street, Santa Barbara
(805) 963-5000
www.palacegrill.com

Piatti's

Dine *al fresco* next to the seasonal live creek on one of two private patios. Kids enjoy watching the pizza's being prepared and wood-fired in the open pizza ovens.

Hours: Sun-Thu 11:30am-9pm, Fri-Sat 11:30am-10pm

Contact Info: 516 San Ysidro Road, Montecito
(805) 969-7520
www.piatti.com

Zookers Café

The down-to-earth approach at this American eatery makes it popular with families. The cuisine is delicious and kid's menu is varied. Local farm-grown produce is featured and desserts are not to be missed!

Hours: Mon-Sat Lunch 1:30-3pm, Dinner 5-9:30pm

Contact Info: 5404 Carpinteria Avenue, Carpinteria
(805) 684-8893
www.zookerscafe.com

TREATS AND SWEETS

Cold Stone Creamery

If you aren't blessed with this creamery in your own home town, then come visit this one in ours. By mixing nuts, fruits and candy into creamy ice cream on a frozen granite stone, it is more like ice cream art.

Hours: Sun-Thu 11am-10pm, Fri-Sat 11am-11pm

Contact Info: 504 State Street, Santa Barbara - (805) 882-9128
5718 Calle Real Road, Goleta - (805) 692-1598
www.coldstonecreamery.com

Crushcakes Cupcakery

Doesn't everyone love cupcakes? Step into Santa Barbara's very own cupcakery and delight your senses with flavor selections such as Lemon Drop, Peanut Butter Cup and Vanilla Harmony. Yum!

Hours: Call

Contact Info: 1315 Anacapa Street, Santa Barbara
(805)963-9353
www.crushcakes.com

McConnells Creamery

Regarded by some critics as the best ice cream in the country, McConnells distributes their product on a nationwide level. Come visit the downtown ice cream parlor off the same street where it was founded, Mission Street, over 50 years ago. Your kids will need no other distraction than a deliciously rich ice cream scoop.

Hours: Mon-Sun 11am-11:30pm

Contact Info: 201 West Mission Street, Santa Barbara
(805) 569-2323

7034 Market Place Drive, Goleta, CA 93117
(805) 968-0780
www.mcconnells.com

Sweet Alley

When it is time to reward your children with a treat, stroll down to Sweet Alley on downtown State Street. This candy wonderland features treats for kids of all ages, and parents too! Enjoy a frozen yogurt or ice cream on a hot summer day. Treat the family to an anticipated break from your downtown shopping spree.

Hours: Sun-Wed 11:30am-9pm, Thu-Sat 11:30am-10pm

Contact Info: 1103A State Street
(805) 899-8304
www.sweet-alley.com

The Great Pacific Ice Cream Store

Mother Stearns Old Fashioned Candy Store

The Santa Barbara pier would not be complete without a candy store and ice cream outlet. Sure to make your visit to the wharf a screaming success, Mother Stearns carries unlimited varieties of candy, from old-fashioned hard candies to 25 different flavors of saltwater taffy. If that isn't enough, indulge the family at The Great Pacific Ice Cream Store with 32- flavors of fine ice cream and sherbet, hand made locally.

Contact Info: End of State Street on Stearn's Wharf
www.stearnswharf.org

Robitailles Candy Shop

Famous for their mints, this candy shop has made all its' candy onsite for over 40 years. There are few homemade candy stores of this nature remaining, and this one is worth a visit.

Hours: Mon-Sat 10-5, Sun 10-3

Contact Info: 900 Linden Avenue, Carpinteria
(805) 684-9340
www.robitaillescandies.com

DELIVERY

The Dining Car

This service delivers select local restaurant food to Santa Barbara, Montecito, Goleta, Carpinteria & beyond. If you want to sample local fare within the confines of your nest, then give them a call.

Contact Info: (805) 898-9669, (888) 472-1953
www.dining-car.com

Pizza Mizza

Gourmet pizza delivered directly to your location. But wait, it doesn't end with pizza... there are wonderfully unique salads and sandwiches available as well – even desserts, wine and beer! In addition, you can have a DVD rental delivered to you along with your order.

Hours: Daily 11a.m. – 9pm

Contact Info: 140 S. Hope Avenue (805) 564-3900
Delivery to Santa Barbara, Goleta,
(805)566-3900 Delivery to Montecito,
Summerland, Carpinteria
www.pizzamizza.com

Chocolate Cake Cafe

What is more outrageous than a succulent chocolate cake delivered directly to your door! Children's packages are available which include balloons, decorated cupcakes and a special cake for the birthday boy/girl. Indulge mom with the vacation package, complete with Pina Coladas and a tropical bouquet.

Contact Info: (805) 969-3174

www.chocolatecakecafe.com

Places To Shop

GROCERIES

Gelson's Super Market

Gelson's has served Southern California customers since 1951. Popular with the community, they feature good traditional American fare for the family. Their hot deli counter packs a super take-out kids meal, complete with a toy gift inside.

Hours: Daily 7am-10pm

Contact Info: 3305 State Street

(805) 687-5810

www.Gelsons.com

Lazy Acres Market

Extremely popular with the local community, this is Santa Barbara's broadest selection of natural, wholesome and organic food and produce. The bakery and deli café are filled with tempting delights. The sandwiches are fabulous for a picnic or just stay in the café to enjoy.

Hours: Daily 7am-10pm

Contact Info: 302 Meigs Road, Santa Barbara

(805) 564-4410

www.LazyAcres.com

Ralphs Fresh Fare

Traditional Super Market in the downtown Santa Barbara area, including pharmacy.

Hours: Daily 24 hours

Contact Info: 100 W.Carrillo Street — (805) 564-7000,
Pharmacy — (805) 564-7070
www.ralphs.com

Santa Barbara Farmers Market

Each week the farmers in the marketplace display a colorful bounty of agricultural products grown in the Santa Barbara County. Seasonal diversity is available year round rain or shine. Music and entertainment enlivens the markets while creating an upbeat ambiance. Markets open 7 days a week at different locations between Carpinteria and Solvang… see web site for specific locations and hours.

Contact Info: (805) 962-5354
www.sbfarmersmarket.org

Tri-County Produce

A wonderful array of local produce as well as shelves and freezers fully stocked with wholesome goodness. The market is guided by their motto: "If it's any fresher, it's still in the fields".

Hours: Daily 9am-7:30pm

Contact Info: 335 South Milpas, Santa Barbara
(805) 965-4558
www.tricountyproduce.com

CLOTHING & ACCESSORIES

Adorably Local

Want something special from Santa Barbara for the wee one? Visit this web site before, after or during your stay for a unique shirt from your adventure in Santa Barbara. Local artists expressly design the selections, and the styles and materials are as high quality and organic as you would expect from this town.

Contact Info: www.adorablylocal.com

Big Dog Sportswear

Big Dog Sportswear is a national branded retailer headquartered in Santa Barbara. Best known for activewear, casual sportswear, gifts and accessories, Big Dogs guarantees Quality-Value-Fun for the entire family, even your dog!

Hours: Mon-Sat 9:30-8pm, Sun 9:30-6pm

Contact Info: 136 State Street Santa Barbara
(805) 963-8728
www.bigdogs.com

Blue Bee Kids

Jump into this store for the most unique and hip kids couture around town. Blue Bee is known in Santa Barbara for its fun contemporary designer collections.

Hours: Mon-Sat 10-6, Sun 11-6

Contact Info: 9 E. Figueroa Street
(805) 965-1956 ext 4
www.bluebeeonline.com

Gap Kids

You are sure to find most basics for your child's wardrobe, and then some, at this national retailer. Located in Paseo Nuevo Mall.

Hours: M-F 10-9, Sat 10-8, Sun 11-7

Contact Info: 617 Paseo Nuevo, Santa Barbara
(805) 899-9124
www.gapkids.com

Gymboree

This popular national retailer offers colorful twists to otherwise ordinary clothing lines. Located in La Cumbre Plaza.

Hours: M-F 10-9, Sat 10-7, Sun 11-6

Contact Info: 3815 State Street, #134, Santa Barbara
(805) 682-7773
www.gymboree.com

Janie and Jack

Merchandising lusciously detailed clothing for your little blossom, this store can be found nationwide. Located in La Cumbre Plaza.

Hours: M-F 10-9, Sat 10-7, Sun 11-6

Contact Info: 110 S. Hope Avenue, Santa Barbara
(805) 682-7012
www.janieandjack.com

K. Frank

The owners of this boutique have taken their collective love of fashion and brought to Santa Barbara a distinctive array of apparel for mom, dad and baby.

Hours: M-Thu 10-6, Sat 10-7, Sun 11-6

Contact Info: 1023 State Street, Santa Barbara
(805) 560-7424
www.kfrankstyle.com

Lamonts Gift Shop at the Four Seasons Biltmore Resort

Those in search of "Santa Barbara" logo'd shirts, caps, and gifts for the kids should come take a peek inside this gift shop at the Biltmore Resort. The Santa Barbara imprinted clothing is thoughtfully selected, and you cannot beat these hours if you are in search of last minute, late night shopping.

Hours: Sun-Fri 7am-10pm, Sat 7am-11pm

Contact Info: 1260 Channel Drive, Montecito
(805) 969-2261

Lucky Kid

Rooted in rock 'n 'roll with a signature style, Lucky Kid is a cheeky children's line brought to us by Lucky Brand Jeans, for kids 6 months to 10 years.

Hours: M-Sat 10-9, Sun 10-7

Contact Info: 740 State Street, Santa Barbara
(805) 966-0272
www.luckybrandjeans.com

Naartjie

Walk into this store and experience the vivid array of soft, comfortable, whimsical garments. The styles are seasonal and unique. Located on downtown State Street, their children's sizes range from 0-8.

Hours: M-Sat 10-7, Sun 11-6

Contact Info: 933 State Street, Santa Barbara
(805) 965-9870
www.naartjie.com

Nordstrom

Located in the Paseo Nuevo Shopping Mall, Nordstrom is a nationwide fashion specialty chain with renowned services, generous size ranges and a selection of the finest apparel, shoes and accessories for the entire family.

Hours: M-F 10-9pm, Sat 10-8, Sun 11-6

Contact Info: 17 W. Canon Perdido, Santa Barbara
(805) 564-8770
www.nordstrom.com

Polar Bear

Kids grow so quickly that a great deal of their clothing, toys, and gear remains in perfect condition once they grow out of it. For this reason, there is Polar Bear. Come here when you are looking to buy (or sell) gently used items that have a great deal of life left.

Hours: M-Sat 10-5, Sun 12-4

Contact Info: 726 Anacapa Street, Santa Barbara
(805) 965-6637

This Little Piggy Wears Cotton

This store features high quality European and domestic merchandise for newborns to age twelve including toys, books, and one-of-a-kind gifts. Choose from brands such as Petit Bateau, Burberry, Juicy Couture and their own PiggyBrand. Located in the Paseo Nuevo Shopping Mall.

Hours: M-F 10-9, Sat 10-8, Sun 11-6

Contact Info: 311 Paseo Nuevo, Santa Barbara
(805)899-2570
www.LittlePiggy.com

Upstairs at Pierre Lafond

Offering a small but extremely specialized and distinctive selection, this Montecito boutique has been selling children's apparel and gifts upstairs for almost 25 years. Sizes range from newborn up to size 6.

Hours: Daily 9am-8pm

Contact Info: 516 San Ysidro Road, Montecito
(805) 565-1503
www.upstairsatpierrelafond.com

Brooks Shoes For Kids

Choose from a selection of shoes, slippers, ballet & tap shoes, backpacks, lunch boxes, hosiery and hair accessories in this LaCumbre Mall store. Shoe sizes range from newborn-10 year olds.

Hours: M-F 10-9, Sat 10-7, Sun 11-6

Contact Info: 3825 State Street, Santa Barbara
(805) 682-2232
www.BrooksShoesforKids.com

Global Feet Kids

This trendy retail store carries styles from premier footwear brands such Pony, Diesel, Naturino, Primigi, Aster, Flacotto, Mode 8, Fancy Feet, and Kinderland. Located on downtown State Street, the location is ideal for strolling.

Hours: M-F 10-7, Sat 10:30-7, Sun 11-6

Contact Info: 939 State Street, Santa Barbara
(805) 957-1910

BABY GEAR AND FURNITURE

Chicken Little

This retailer on downtown State Street carries a wide variety of well-known brands, as well as a variety of specialty items just for the Santa Barbara patron.

Hours: M-Sat 10-6, Sun 10:30-5:30

Contact Info: 1236 State Street, Santa Barbara
(805) 962-7771
www.chickenlittlekids.com

Mon Petite Bijou

A grand presentation of fine quality products, this two-story location prides itself on customer service. Here you will find an extensive collection of upscale clothing, furniture, equipment and accessories for your child.

Hours: M-Sat 10-6, Sun 11-5

Contact Info: 922 State Street, Santa Barbara
(800) 945-0015
www.monpetitbijou.com

Santa Barbara Baby Furniture and Accessories

Family owned for over 15 years, this retailer is well known for their exceptionally friendly service. The store has the best prices in town for brand named baby and toddler equipment and accessories. Cross the street to Santa Barbara's own McConnells Creamery for a special treat after shopping.

Hours: M-F 10:30-6, Sat 11-6

Contact Info: 1936 De La Vina Street, Santa Barbara
(805) 682-7517

TOYS, ART & GAMES

Bennetts Educational Materials

The educational supplies here range from traditional classroom supplies to quality toys, games, art supplies, books, and much more. Come here for a unique children's gift.

Hours: M-F 9:30-6:30, Sat 9-5:30, Sun 1-5

Contact Info: 5130 Hollister Avenue, Santa Barbara
(805) 964 8998
www.bennettseducational.com

Craft Essentials

Kids craft supplies range from beads, frames, sewing and candles to all sorts of art supplies.

Hours: M-F 9-8, Sat 9-7, Sun 10-6

Contact Info: 187 Turnpike Road, Santa Barbara
(805) 681-3115

Discovery Channel Store

This Paseo Nuevo Mall store offers educational toys and games to spark the imagination, toys that help children of all ages learn and grow, and a wide selection of remote control toys great for indoor or outdoor play.

Hours: M-F 10-9, Sat 10-8, Sun 11-7

Contact Info: 209 Paseo Nuevo, Santa Barbara
(805) 564-1918
www.discoverychannelstore.com

Game-Seeker

Home to a large selection of games, puzzles and gifts that help stimulate the mind. Kids of all ages can choose from an array of traditional board games and puzzles to card and electronic games.

Hours: Sun-Fri 11:30-6, Fri-Sat 11:30-9pm

Contact Info: 537 State Street, Santa Barbara
(805) 564-6611
www.game-seeker.com

KB Toys

This national retailer strives to offer friendly, efficient service with a wide selection of toys and good values. Located in La Cumbre Plaza.

Hours: M-F 10-9, Sat 10-7, Sun 11-6

Contact Info: 136 S Hope Avenue # 47, Santa Barbara
(805) 682-6026
www.kbtoys.com

Kernohan's Toys

A Santa Barbara original since 1954, this toy store offers "the finest toys for the finest kids". Themes include science, construction, crafts, and music.

Hours: M-Thu 10-6, Fir 10-7, Sat 10-6, Sun 12-5

Contact Info: 5739 Calle Real, Goleta
(805) 964-6499
www.kernohanstoys.com

Michaels

With hundreds of stores throughout North America, this national retailer sells almost any art and craft supply you can think up.

Hours: M-Sat 9-9, Sun 10-7

Contact Info: 187 N Fairview Ave, Goleta
(805) 967-7119
www.michaels.com

SB Museum of Art-Store

Here you will find children's toys and games that are imaginative and artistic in nature. Selections include creative Klutz Kits, Anatex wooden toys, Eeboo & Mudpuppy learning games along with Alex painting & craft activity kits.

Hours: M-Sat 10-6, Sun 11-5

Contact Info: 1130 State Street, Santa Barbara
(805) 884-6454
www.sbma.net

Santa Barbara Scrapbooks

For those looking to preserve the photos from their coastal adventure, this is our local full service scrapbooking and paper arts center.

Hours: Mon-Sat 10-7, Sun 12-7

Contact Info: 918 Chapala Street, Santa Barbara
(805) 962-5099
www.sbscarpbooks.com

The Great American General Store

For those in search of novelty toys, fun clothing and books that will make you smile, step into this charismatic store. You are sure to find a unique gift for kids of all ages.

Hours: Tues-Sun 10-5

Contact Info: 9th Avenue, Carpinteria
(805) 684-0400
www.greatamericangeneralstore.com

SHOPPING MALLS

La Cumbre Plaza

One of Santa Barbara's largest shopping malls is La Cumbre Plaza. It includes two department stores, Macys and Sears, Vons Grocery, and more than 60 shops, restaurants, services and easy parking.

Hours: M-F 10-9, Sat 10-7, Sun 11-6

Contact Info: 121 S. Hope Avenue, Santa Barbara
(805) 687-6458
www.shoplacumbre.com

Paseo Nuevo Shopping Mall

Paseo Nuevo Mall includes Nordstrom, Macys, and more than 50 specialty shops and movie theaters. The kids can run around outside and have fun throwing coins into the fountain. If you don't want to walk the whole length of State Street with the kids, then hop on the shuttle or one of the pedi-cabs. This is a blast for the kids.

Hours: M-F 9am-9pm, Sat 10-8, Sun 11-6

Contact Info: 651 Paseo Nuevo, Santa Barbara
(805) 963-7147
www.sbmall.com

Camino Real Marketplace

Come here if you are in search of the familiar, national super stores such as Linens 'n' Things, Costco, Staples, Sports Authority and Home Depot. There are also a handful of local establishments such as McConnell's Ice Cream and Blenders in the Grass, as well as a large Metropolitan movie theater.

Contact Info: Marketplace Drive, Goleta
(805) 685-3458
www.caminorealmarketplace.com

Places To Sleep

T he recommendations in this section are based on accommodations that provide extra amenities for children and families, such as separate sleeping quarters for the kids, kitchenettes, and proximity to activities. For Rustic Camping and Cabin accommodations, please see the Outdoors section of this book.

If you are need of assistance with choosing a motel or hotel, contact the local specialists at **Hot Spots** – (800)793-7666 or www.hotspotsusa.com.

MOTELS, HOTELS, and INNS

Ala Mar Motel

This charming motel also rents out a few one-bedroom apartments just down the street from the beach and motel. They are equipped with a full kitchen and queen bed in the living room, king bed in the bedroom.

Contact Info: 102 W Cabrillo Blvd, Santa Barbara
(805) 962-9208
www.alamarmotel.com

Blue Sands Motel

This simple, family-owned and operated motel is a convenient beachside location at an affordable price. A few of the rooms have kitchens with a separate bedroom.

Contact Info: 421 South Milpas Street, Santa Barbara
(805) 965-1624
www.bluesandsmotel.com

Brisas Del Mar, Inn at the Beach

Just two blocks from the beach and harbor, this Mediterranean style inn offers suites with full kitchens. The heated pool is well groomed, as is the entire landscape. A deluxe continental breakfast and afternoon wine reception with evening milk and cookies adds a nice touch for the parents and children alike.

Contact Info: 223 Castillo Street, Santa Barbara
(805) 966-2219
www.sbhotels.com

Cabrillo Inn

Relax and enjoy spectacular ocean and island views from your room, by the pool, or one of the second floor sundecks. This motel sits directly across the street from the beach. They also rent Spanish vacation cottages by the week.

Contact Info: 931 East Cabrillo Blvd, Santa Barbara
(800) 648-6708
www.cabrillo-inn.com

Casa Del Mar

This seaside Inn is charming in every respect. Many of the suites and rooms are fully equipped with kitchens, and fire-places. As opposed to a traditional Bed and Breakfast, all the guest rooms have private, courtyard entrances.

Contact Info: 18 Bath Street, Santa Barbara
(800) 433-3097
www.casadelmar.com

Coast Village Inn

If you are looking to stay in exclusive Montecito, this location is ideal. Some of these thoughtfully appointed suites and rooms include kitchenettes.

Contact Info: 1188 Coast Village Road, Montecito
(800) 257-5131
www.coastvillageinn.com

Franciscan Inn

Originally a Spanish-style ranch house from the 1920's, this Spanish-Mediterranean hideaway is just one block from the beach and next door to a quiet residential area. The suites have kitchenettes.

Contact Info: 109 Bath Street, Santa Barbara
(805) 963-8845
www.franciscaninn.com

Harbor House Inn

Located one short block from the beach, the Harbor House is a small, unique inn. All guest rooms are studios with complete small kitchens. The welcome breakfast basket upon arrival is an added treat!

Contact Info: 104 Bath Street, Santa Barbara
(805) 962-9745
www.harborhouseinn.com

Harbor View Inn

While the suites offer a separate bedroom, only the ocean view suites at this beachside resort can accommodate the toddler cots and cribs that are provided via the hotel. The fitness room is an added bonus, and the location is nicely situated between Stearns Wharf and the harbor.

Contact Info: 28 W. Cabrillo Blvd., Santa Barbara
(800) 755-0222
www.harborviewinnsb.com

Inn at East Beach

The Inn enjoys a tranquil location, convenient to shopping, dining, and the Wharf. Just steps away form the beach, this hotel offers kitchen suites and a heated pool.

Contact Info: 1029 Orilla Del Mar, Santa Barbara
(800) 575-5667
www.innateastbeach.com

Marina Beach Motel

This well manicured motel is just steps away from the beach, and offers a complimentary continental breakfast, as well as use of bikes. Kitchenettes are available.

Contact Info: 21 Bath Street, Santa Barbara
(877)627-4621
www.marinabeachmotel.com

Mason Beach Inn

Just one block from the beach and the West beach playground, Mason Beach Inn is affordable, friendly and offers suites with kitchenettes. It is also walking distance to the Harbor and various restaurants.

Contact Info: 324 W. Mason Street, Santa Barbara
(800) 446-0444
www.masonbeachinn.com

The Beach House Inn and Apartments

If you are looking for some elbow room, look no further. The family suites, double studios and apartment offer family comfort features such as kitchens, separate bedrooms, patios. The location is a few blocks from the beach and harbor. Pets are OK here.

Contact Info: 320 W. Yanonali Street, Santa Barbara
(805) 966-1126
www.thebeachhouseinn.com

Best Western Carpinteria Inn

If you are looking for a convenient place to lay your head in Carpinteria, this could be your best choice. While this afford-able Inn only has 2 suites with a full kitchen, it also has a Grille on site.

Contact Info: 4558 Carpinteria Avenue, Carpinteria
(805) 684-0473
www.bestwestern.com

The Villas at Hotel MarMonte

Separate from the hotel, the Villas are designed to offer guests with an apartment-style setting. The most attractive quality about the Villas is the total access to the Hotel Mar Monte's full service property, featuring an outdoor pool and Jacuzzi, ocean-front fitness center, restaurant, a gift shop for necessities and a spa.

Contact Info: 1111 East Cabrillo Blvd, Santa Barbara
(805) 963-0744
www.hotelmarmonte.com

Summer Inn Santa Barbara on UCSB campus

This option is only available to groups and families with a minimum of 15 people needed to make a reservation. Only open for two months during the summer, the Summer Inn capacity is 60 people. Amenities include kitchen, lounge and laundry facilities.

Contact Info: (805) 893-2649
www.summerinnsantabarbara.com

Family Vacation Center on UCSB Campus

This residential resort on the UCSB campus offers diverse recreational and social activities for the whole family. The package price includes all meals, lodging with daily housekeeping service, and most activities. Children participate in activities with kids their own age, under supervision of enthusiastic UCSB student counselors. They offer childcare programs for children under two, while providing exciting activities for the more demanding teenager. Eight one-week sessions are offered yearly during the months of July and August. Families attend for a minimum of one week at a time.

Contact Info: (805) 893-3123

www.familyvacationcenter.com

RESORTS

The Alisal Guest Ranch and Resort

Guest units are decorated in classic California ranch design. Delicious cuisine in a ranch-style dining room is also included in the price of your stay. Activities for children include a Petting Zoo with an assortment of ranch animals, an arts and crafts program and lessons in fishing, boating and swimming. Horseback riding, golf and tennis lessons are offered to children seven years old and over.

Contact Info: 1054 Alisal Road, Solvang

(805) 688-6411

www.alisal.com

Bacara Resort and Spa

This Mediterranean style resort boasts a full service spa, restaurant, bar, pools & cabana, golf, and beach access. The Bacara Kid's Club is available daily to any guest with children between the ages 5 to 12. Special evening programs and activities are offered during holiday weekends. Advanced reservations for the Kids Club are suggested.

Contact Info: 8301 Hollister Avenue, Santa Barbara
(805) 968-0100, (877) 422-4245
www.bacararesort.com

Fess Parkers Doubletree Resort

This resort is centrally located, directly across from the beach and along the popular Cabrillo Boulevard. Many local attractions are just a stroll away, such as the wharf, sea center, zoo, restaurants, activity rentals and harbor shuttle. There is a café inside the hotel as well as a coffee kiosk for those lazy days by the pool. The hotel hosts organized activities for kids during the summer season from July through September, and you can rent surreys (multiple-seater bikes) directly at the hotel.

Contact Info: 633 East Cabrillo Boulevard, Santa Barbara
(805) 564-4333
www.fpdtr.com

Four Seasons Biltmore Resort

A Spanish colonial treasure located across from the beautiful Butterfly Beach in exclusive Montecito, this classic resort offers a Kids for All Seasons program for children ages 4 and older – be sure to confirm availability during your stay. The guest accommodations (rooms, suites and 12 private cottages) are all located on the palm-tree lined, sprawling grounds that comprise this elegant resort.

Contact Info: 1260 Channel Drive, Santa Barbara
(805) 969-2261
www.fourseasons.com/santabarbara

RANCH STYLE LODGING

San Ysidro Ranch

A Rosewood Resort property, the San Ysidro Ranch is an historic retreat for the discriminating travelers. The secluded acreage is nestled in the luxurious Montecito foothills. The cottages and two-bedroom studios are the best options for families. There are two restaurants onsite and a nearby village. Choose this resort when you would like privacy and pampering.

Contact Info: 900 San Ysidro Lane, Santa Barbara
  (805)565-1700
  www.sanysidroranch.com

HOUSE AND CONDO RENTALS

Many families find the most comfort staying in a home, especially for long-term visits. Below are prominent home rental agencies to select from. For extra comfort, furnish the home with a crib, toddler bed, high chair, toys, and such... visit Santa Barbara Baby Company for your rental needs at: www.SBBabyCo.com or call (805) 275-2414.

Santa Barbara Luxury Rentals

Professionally managed luxury rental properties
(800) 381-0964
www.sbluxuryrentals.com

Coastal Hideaways

Great service for those looking to rent a coastal hideaway
(805)569-6571
www.coastalhideaways.com

Coastal Properties

Full service real estate company offering premier property rental
(805) 969-1258
www.coastalrealty.com

Vacation Homes

Homes for rent across the nation, as well as internationally
www.vacationhomes.com

Vacation Rental By Owner

Vacation home rentals listed by owners and property
managers
www.vrbo.com

Vacation Rental Postings

See link for Vacation Rentals under Housing Section
http://santabarbara.craigslist.org

SPECIAL SERVICES FOR PARENTS

Anacapa Cleaning

For those visitors who need a helping hand while in town.
Why not vacation with the luxury of not cleaning up. Anacapa
Cleaning specializes in vacation rental cleaning. This is your
time off as parents so enjoy it!

Contact Info: (805) 886-8155

www.anacapacleaning.com

Early Life Photography

Educated at the UCLA School of Design and the Brooks Institute
of Photography, Medeighnia Lentz specializes in early life
documentation as a career. Her photography is a celebration

of life. Capture the beauty of your children at this special moment in Santa Barbara… you'll treasure these photographs for a lifetime.

Contact Info: (805) 452-3462

www.earlylifephotography.com (805) 452-3462

Jelly Photography

Why not take advantage of the spectacular coastline and take a professional photo of your child while you are in town! John Ellis specializes in photojournalistic style photography - candid and expressive, utilizing natural light and settings.

Contact Info: (805) 637-4776

www.jellyphotography.com

Mummy's Day Off

These caring, fun and responsible sitters are available for you in the Santa Barbara area. Their sitters are carefully screened, have references, and are CPR certified. They encourage you to call anytime - 24 hours a day.

Contact Info: (805) 571-6171

www.mummysdayoff.com

Child Time

This licensed and bonded nanny placement service offers hotel and residential on call service.

Contact Info: (805) 729-5460

www.childtimenanny.com

Kids Cuts

With a playroom full of toys and videos, your child will hardly notice the hair cut. It is more difficult to leave than to enter this place.

Contact Info: 4317 State Street, Santa Barbara
(805)681-9596

The Tortoise and the Hair

Need a haircut in town for the kids? Designed specifically for kids, this downtown salon has a playroom and many natural grooming products for sale.

Contact Info: 726 State Street, Santa Barbara
(805) 963-3393

The Little Guest

Guests and hosts can relax at special occasions with all the children professionally cared for - right on site! Bubbles, beanbags, balls, and beads are just a part of the action. Experienced and licensed staff arrive early to set up the specially designated area filled with professionally supervised, age-appropriate games and crafts.

Contact Info: (805) 688-1812
www.thelittleguest.com –

Seasonal Festivals and Activities

Annual Events By Month

Santa Barbara residents thirst for both cultural stimulus and an active lifestyle. In turn, the city is ripe with festivals, events, shows and activities. On any given weekend you should be able to choose from events at a city park, the zoological gardens, Earl Warren Showgrounds, Ty Warner Sea Center, Natural History Museum, or any one of the other historical grounds.

Please contact the venue for specific time and dates for the event. Event dates and months will fluctuate every year, and we have listed our best estimation of occurrence, based on previous years.

January

Date	Event	Venue	Town
Mid-January	International Percussion Festival	Various	Santa Barbara
Late January-Early February	Super Saturday	South Coast Railroad Museum	Goleta
Late January-Early February	International Film Festival	Various Downtown Locations	Santa Barbara

International Percussion Festival

This week full of performances and clinics is filled with events for the kids, from interactive shows to clinics, and more. Sponsored by the Santa Barbara Symphony.

Contact Info: 1900 State Street Suite G, Santa Barbara
(805) 898-9626
www.thesymphony.org

Annual Super Saturday!

The Annual ""Super Saturday!"" will be held at the museum on the day before the Super Bowl football game. The event marks the first weekend day of unlimited free miniature-train rides during the new year. It is open to the general public.

Venue: South Coast Railroad Museum

Contact Info: 300 North Los Carneros Road, Goleta
(805) 964-3540
www.goletadepot.org

Santa Barbara International Film Festival

Hailed as a premier film festival on the West Coast, this event accommodates kids with family friendly programming held on specific mornings, usually weekends. Now you can participate in the screenings without needing a sitter.

Contact Info: 1528 Chapala Street, Suite 203, Santa Barbara
(805) 963-0023
www.sbfilmfestival.org

February

Date	Event	Venue	Town
Late January- Early February	Super Saturday	South Coast Railroad Museum	Goleta
Late January- Early February	International Film Festival	Various Downtown Locations	Santa Barbara
Early February	Valentines Nature Craft Workshop	Santa Barbara Botanic Gardens	Santa Barbara

Annual Super Saturday!
See January Section

Santa Barbara International Film Festival
See January Section

Valentine's Nature Craft Workshop

This parent-child workshop held at the Santa Barbara Botanic Garden will have the family working together to create greeting cards, wreaths, and Valentines ornaments using natural materials.

Contact Info: 1212 Mission Canyon Road, Santa Barbara
(805) 682-4726
www.sbbg.org

March

Date	Event	Venue	Town
Early March	Celebration of the Whales Festival	Channel Islands Harbor	Oxnard
Mid March	Kids Fishing Day	Lake Casitas	Ventura

Annual Celebration of the Whales Festival

This festival highlights the migration of the Pacific Gray Whale from Alaska to Mexico. Activities include whale & marine education exhibits, tide pool touch tank aboard the "coral sea", children's games & activities including "whale of a treasure hunt", and whale drawing coloring contest, free balloons, face painting, gigantic inflatable fun zone and rock climbing wall.

Venue: Channel Islands Harbor, Oxnard

Contact Info: 2741 South Victoria Avenue, Oxnard
(805) 985-4852
www.channelislandsharbor.org

Kid's Fishing Day

Lake Casitas Recreation Park holds this day as a way of encouraging youngsters (of all ages) to get up close and personal with the fish. Along with a live fish plant in the lake, learning stations are set up with fish for the children to catch, a free "goodie" bag while supplies last, and to round it off, and a free Hot Dog lunch for the first 200 registered kids.

Contact Info: 11311 Santa Ana Road, Ventura
(805) 649-2233
www.LakeCasitas.info

April

Date	Event	Venue	Town
Early-Mid April	Spring Egg Hunt	Botanic Garden	Santa Barbara
Early-Mid April	Easter Lunch	Fillmore Railway	Fillmore
Early-Mid April	Egg Hunt	Elings Park	Santa Barbara
Early-Mid April	Egg Hunt and Eggstravaganza	Hans Christian Anderson Park	Solvang
Mid April	Kite Festival	City College	Santa Barbara
Mid April	Kids Draw Architecture	Courthouse & Presidio	Santa Barbara
Mid April	Santa Barbara Founding Day	El Presidio	Santa Barbara
Mid-Late April	Day Out with Thomas the Train	Fillmore Railway	Fillmore
Late April	Santa Barbara Faire and Expo	Earl Warren Showgrounds	Santa Barbara
Late April	Earth Day	Courthouse Gardens	Santa Barbara
Late April	Sea Festival	Maritime Museum	Santa Barbara
Late April	Strawberry Festival	Santa Maria Fairpark	Santa Maria

Santa Barbara Botanic Garden Annual Spring Egg Hunt

An afternoon of egg hunting and crafts for children ages 3-10.

Contact Info: 1212 Mission Canyon Road, Santa Barbara
(805) 682-4726
www.sbbg.org

Easter Lunch at the Fillmore Railway Company

Enjoy a 2 1/2 hour scenic train ride and a visit from the Easter bunny.

Contact Info: 250 Central Ave, Fillmore
(800) 773-8724
www.fwry.com

Egg Hunt at Elings Park

The egg hunts are divided into 3 age groups (for 10 and under). A Bouncer and other activities include photo opportunities with the Easter Bunny! Bring a basket.

Contact Info: Elings Park, Santa Barbara
(805) 569-5611
www.elingspark.org

Annual Easter Egg Hunt and Eggstravaganza at Hans Christian Anderson Park

Contests and games include the bunny hop race and jelly bean relay. A BBQ and face painting add to the delight. Bring a basket for the morning egg hunt.

Contact Info: Solvang Visitors Center
(800) 468-6765
www.cityofsolvang.com

Santa Barbara Kite Festival

Competitive kite flying joins up with food and games to create a kite flying burlesque. Go to the Great Meadow on the West Campus Lawn.

Contact Info: Santa Barbara City College, 721 Cliff Drive,
Santa Barbara
(800) 682-2895
www.sbkitefest.com

Annual Kids Draw Architecture

Children sketch Santa Barbara's famous landmark buildings, guided by local architects and design professionals who offer encouragement and creative direction to these young artists during outdoor drawing sessions. Sketches are later featured in a gallery and calendar. See website for dates and locations.

Contact Info: Santa Barbara Courthouse & El Presidio
(805) 965-6307
www.afsb.org

Santa Barbara Founding Day

This educational event offers a variety of engaging activities that shed light on the history of early California. Living History Demonstrations, Adobe Brick Making, Ceramics, Archaeology, and dance performances are all a part of the festivities.

Contact Info: El Presidio, 123 E. Canon Perdido Street,
Santa Barbara
(805) 966-9719
www.sbthp.org

Day Out with Thomas the Train

Children and their grownups take a 25-minute ride with Thomas the Tank Engine™ and have their picture taken with Sir Topham Hatt™, the Superintendent of the Railroad. Activities include Thomas & Friends™ storytelling, a viewing station for Thomas & Friends videos, temporary tattoos, an Imagination Station.

Contact Info: Fillmore Railway Co., 250 Central Avenue,
Fillmore
(800) 773-8724
www.fwry.com

Annual Santa Barbara Fair & Expo

Offering fun and excitement for the entire family, this fair has something for everyone… thrill-seeker rides, the Giant Wheel, a Carousel, interactive exhibits for kids, puppet shows, crafts, and much more. Magicians and hypnotists astonish passers-by with their tricks, and local singers, dancers and musicians entertain fair-goers with their performances. The annual competition for the best local foods, wine and beer, arts & crafts, horticulture and fine arts draws a crowd. The kids always want a close-up view of the large and small livestock competitions as they are presented in showground arenas.

Contact Info: Earl Warren Showgrounds, U.S. Hwy 101
at Las Positas Exit
(805) 687-0766
www.sbfairandexpo.com

Earth Day Festival

Santa Barbara's Earth Day festival features over 130 booths. Highlights include a children's activity area, live music from the solar-powered stage, a healthy food court, free bicycle check-ups, an energy village, a Green Car Show.

Contact Info: Courthouse Gardens, 1100 Anacapa Street,
Santa Barbara
(805)963-0583 ext.109
www.communityenvironmentalcouncil.org

Seasonal Festivals and Activities

Annual Sea Festival

Santa Barbara Maritime Museum hosts its' annual Sea Festival to celebrate and showcase the visiting tall ship, Spirit of Dana Point. Maritime activities include public dockside tours and sailing aboard the tall ship, ROV (Remotely Operated Vehicle) and hardhat diving demonstrations, craft activities, marine life touch tank, storytelling, and more!

Contact Info: 113 Harbor Way, Suite 190, Santa Barbara
(805) 962-8404 ext.115
www.sbmm.org

Annual Strawberry Festival

What child can resist an enormous strawberry dipped in chocolate, or a strawberry shake or ice cream cone? If you can imagine it in "strawberry", then you will find it here! Enjoy food, fun, rides, and all kinds of family entertainment while paying tribute to the richness of Santa Barbara County's exceptional crop.

Contact Info: Santa Maria Fairpark, 937 S. Thornburg Street,
Santa Maria
(805) 925-8824
www.santamariafairpark.com

May

Date	Event	Venue	Town
May-August	El Capitan Canyon Summer Concerts and BBQ	El Capitan Canyon	Santa Barbara County
May-September	Night Moves	Leadbetter Beach	Santa Barbara
May-September	Fairy Tales in the Park	Various Parks	Ventura County
Early May	Village of Tales	Libbey Bowl	Ojai
Early May	Mothers Day Run & Family Festival	Goleta Beach	Goleta
Early May	Cinco De Mayo Festival	Plaza de la Guerra	Santa Barbara
Mid May	Jewish Festival	Congregation B'nai B'rith	Santa Barbara
Mid May	California Strawberry Festival	Strawberry Meadows of College Park	Oxnard
Memorial Day Weekend	I Madonnari Italian Street Painting Festival	Santa Barbara Mission	Santa Maria

El Capitan Canyon Summer Concerts and Barbecue

Every Saturday at 6 pm, El Capitan Canyon hosts a star filled evening of Blues, Jazz and Bluegrass Music. Families of all ages enjoy outdoor dining and dancing near the creekside. Bring your own picnic dinner or enjoy the popular BBQ dinner option at the facility.

Contact Info: 11560 Calle Real, Santa Barbara County
(866) 352-2729
www.elcapitancanyon.com

Nite Moves

An early evening workout and family party at Leadbetter Beach Park each Wednesday night. Your evening workout can be a vigorous or casual walk, a fun or competitive 5K run, or an ocean swim. There is a soft-sand sprint just for the kids with rewards from McConnells Ice Cream. A featured host serves buffet each week to the tunes of live entertainment. Register on-site.

Contact Info: Leadbetter Beach, Santa Barbara
www.runsantabarbara.com

Fairy Tales in the Park

Since 1995, this all-volunteer troupe of actors have been performing free fairy tales for the young and young at heart all over Ventura County. The goal is to create an environment where families can introduce live theatre to their children in a casual setting at the right price - FREE! See their web site for specific dates and locations.

Contact Info: (661) 718-3968
www.fairytalesinthepark.com

Village of Tales

With a magical setting of peaks and blossoms filling the valley, this Storytelling Festival, hosted by Performance To Grow On, offers captivating performances for all ages. The festival is best suited for families with children ages 5 and up.

Contact Info: Libbey Bowl, Ojai Valley
(805) 646-8907
www.ptgo.org

Mother's Day 5K/10K & Family Festival

SBparent.com and Moms in Motion hosts this scenic run that the whole family can enjoy, plus a Kid's Fun Run. A beachside family festival with kids activities, art and crafts, a silent auction, and much more follows morning runs.

Contact Info: Goleta Beach , Goleta
(805) 448-2426
www.momsinmotion.com & www.sbparent.com

Cinco De Mayo Festival

Come taste the flavor of Santa Barbara's rich Hispanic heritage. Delight in the great music, dance, savory food, and a kids corner full of activities.

Contact Info: (805) 965-8561
www.cincodemayosb.com

Annual Jewish Festival

Experience the rich traditions and culture of the Jewish people on a day filled with dance, food, crafts, art, and music of this joyous culture.

Contact Info: Congregation B'nai B'rith
www.sbjf.org

California Strawberry Festival

This "perfect summer kick-off" benefits the community and honors its' agricultural heritage. Come for a day of strawberries and fun for the entire family, featuring an interactive Star Berry Hunt utilizing clues and prizes.

Contact Info: College Park, Oxnard
(888)288-9242
www.strawberry-fest.org

I Madonnari Italian Street Painting Festival

Witness the transformation of the Old Mission plaza with 200 colorful, large-scale street paintings created by 400 artists and young people. The artists (madonnari) begin working on Saturday morning of the Memorial Day weekend and continue drawing throughout the three-day festival, or until their street paintings are completed.

Contact Info: Santa Barbara Mission, Santa Barbara
(805)964-4710
www.imadonnarifestival.com

June

Date	Event	Venue	Town
May–August	El Capitan Canyon Summer Concerts and BBQ	El Capitan Canyon	Santa Barbara County
May–September	Night Moves	Leadbetter Beach	Santa Barbara
May–September	Fairy Tales in the Park	Various Parks	Ventura County
June–August	Concerts in the Park	Chase Palm Park	Santa Barbara
June–October	Solvang Theaterfest	Festival Theater	Solvang
Early June	Big Dog Parade & Canine Festival	State Street	Santa Barbara
Early June	Bicycle Festival	Elings Park	Santa Barbara
Mid June	Live Oak Music Festival	Hwy 154 near Cachuma Lake	Santa Barbara County
Mid June	Flower Festival	Ryon Park	Lompoc
Late June	Summer Solstice Parade	State Street & Alameda Park	Santa Barbara
Late June – Early July	Semana Nautica	Leadbetter Beach	Santa Barbara

Seasonal Festivals and Activities

El Capitan Canyon Summer Concerts and Barbecue

See May Section

Nite Moves

See May Section

Fairy Tales in the Park

See May Section

Concerts In The Park

If the outdoor music and dancing is not enough to keep the kids entertained, then the adjacent playground is sure to fill in. Pack a picnic dinner, lawn chairs and some blankets and bring the whole family to this wildly popular concert series. There are few venues better than Chase Palm Park with its palm lined, ocean-view amphitheater. Every Thursday evening beginning at 6:30pm.

Contact Info: Chase Palm Park, Santa Barbara
(805) 897-1982
www.sbparksandrecreation.com

Solvang Theaterfest

From Disney to Shakespeare, this 700-seat outdoor facility offers concerts, plays and musicals on a stage under the stars. The Solvang Festival Theater welcomes patrons to come and enjoy the theater grounds before a performance with a picnic and visit with family and friends. Dress in layers for cool evenings…and bring blanket. In order to respect all the attendees in this outdoor venue, the organization respectfully requests that no children under the age of five attend.

Contact Info: Solvang Festival Theater, 420 Second Street,
Solvang
(805) 686-1789
www.solvangtheaterfest.org

Big Dog Parade & Canine Festival

Over 1200 dogs strut down State Street in an attempt to win the Best in Parade, Best Costume, and Most Humorous Parade contests. Join the Canine Festival at Old Chase Palm Park after the parade. The festival includes contests, live music, games, vendor booths, great food, a bounce house and much more.

Contact Info: Big Dogs Corporation
(805) 963-8727
www.bigdogs.com

Annual Santa Barbara Bicycle Festival

A fun-filled day of activity including various BMX and Mountain bike races, a bike swap meet, live music, great food, and a beer garden. Bring your bike ... even if you're not racing!

Contact Info: Elings Park, Jerry Harwin Parkway,
Santa Barbara
(805) 569-5611
www.santabarbarabikefest.com

Live Oak Music Festival

This family event encourages parents to bring their kids. A childcare tent for the evening concerts allows parents to focus on the music. Hands-on arts, crafts and storytelling, talent show, scavenger hunt, and some fun teen activities are just some of the organized activities for kids. They'll be asking to come again next year!

Contact Info: KCBX Public Radio, San Luis Obispo
(805) 781-3020
www.liveoakfest.org

Lompoc Flower Festival

Celebrate the splendor of the colorful Lompoc flower fields at this annual festival. There is a carnival for the kids, as well as a parade, arts and crafts show, food booths, local vendors, and more.

Contact Info: Ryon Park, Lompoc
(805) 735-8511
www.flowerfestival.org

Summer Solstice Parade

Known for its wild variety of floats, giant puppets, and other creative means of transportation, this colorful parade is sure to stimulate the imagination of any child. The parade empties into Alameda Park where the Festival takes place. The Children's Area features storytellers, musicians, drama, mimes and more. Kids can jump on an air bouncer, have their faces painted and work on art projects.

Contact Info: State Street, Santa Barbara
(805) 965-3396
www.solsticeparade.com

Semana Nautica

Santa Barbara's Annual Summer Sports Festival incorporates a series of events over the span of a month. These events range from the extremely physically challenging to those that welcome participants of all ages. Spectators are encouraged to come join the fun. See the web site for detailed event schedules.

Contact Info: (805) 897-2680
www.semananautica.com

July

Date	Event	Venue	Town
May–August	El Capitan Canyon Summer Concerts and BBQ	El Capitan Canyon	Santa Barbara County
May–September	Night Moves	Leadbetter Beach	Santa Barbara
May–September	Fairy Tales in the Park	Various Parks	Ventura County
June–August	Concerts in the Park	Chase Palm Park	Santa Barbara
June–October	Solvang Theaterfest	Festival Theater	Solvang
Late June – Early July	Semana Nautica	Leadbetter Beach	Santa Barbara
July – October	Pick Your Own Berries	Morrell Nut & Berry Farm	Solvang
July	Zoovies	Santa Barbara Zoo	Santa Barbara
July 4th	Independence Day Parade	Linden Avenue	Carpinteria
July 4th	Fireworks by the Sea	Channel Islands Harbor	Oxnard
July 4th	Old Fashioned Fourth of July	Stow House	Goleta
July 4th	Independence Day Celebration	State Street, Chase Palm Park, Harbor	Santa Barbara

Seasonal Festivals and Activities

July *continued*

Date	Event	Venue	Town
July 4th	Fireworks Festival	Girsh Park	Goleta
July 4th	4th of July Street Fair	Main Street	Ventura
Early July	Santa Barbara National Horse Show	Earl Warren Showgrounds	Santa Barbara
Mid-July	French Festival	Oak Park	Santa Barbara
Mid-July	Santa Barbara County Fair	Santa Maria Fairpark	Santa Maria
Late July	Greek Festival	Oak Park	Santa Barbara
Late July	Presidio Pasttimes	Presidio	Santa Barbara
Late July	Summer Celebration and Art Show	Santa Barbara Maritime Museum	Santa Barbara

El Capitan Canyon Summer Concerts and Barbecue
See May Section

Nite Moves
See May Section

Fairy Tales in the Park
See May Section

Concerts In The Park
See June Section

Semana Nautica

See June Section

Solvang Theaterfest

See June Section

Morrell Nut & Berry Farm: Pick Your Own Berries

It's always a good idea for kids to learn that berries don't originate in the super market. Take the family a step back in time and visit one of Solvang's turn-of-the-century properties. Come pick your own raspberries, ollalieberries, and blackberries. Grab a recipe for jam and enjoy the berries all year long. Kids are proud to pack a sandwich for their school lunch that is filled with jam from their own picked berries. Take your freshly-picked basket down the road to The Brothers Restaurant at Mattei's Tavern and the bartender will whip up a berry margarita.

Contact Info: 1980 Alamo Pintado Road, Solvang
(805) 688-8969

Zoovies

Bring your blankets and set your lawn chairs under the stars to enjoy G-rated Hollywood feature films outdoors at the zoo. Movies are offered one night per week throughout the month. Refreshments are available for purchase.

Contact Info: Santa Barbara Zoo, 500 Niños Drive,
Santa Barbara
(805) 962-5339
www.sbzoo.org

Seasonal Festivals and Activities

Independence Day Parade

This parade strolls right down Linden Avenue, downtown main street in Carpinteria. The parade generally occurs the weekend during, or before July 4th.

Contact Info: Linden Avenue, Carpinteria

www.carpcofc.com

Annual Fireworks by the Sea

Join this celebration for a full day of food and fun - Arts & Crafts, Live Music, Food Booths, Water Taxi Rides, Children's Games & Activities, Make Your Own Aquarium, Face Painting & Free Balloons, Gigantic Inflatable Fun Zone, Rock Climbing Wall, Petting Zoo, Pony Rides for the Kids and much more!

Contact Info: Channel Islands Harbor,
2741 South Victoria Avenue, Oxnard
(805) 207-9579
www.channelislandsharbor.org

Old Fashioned 4th of July at Stow House

In addition to the historical park and museum, the festivities include Hay Wagon and Antique Fire Truck rides, games for kids, arts and crafts vendors, antique car show, traditional BBQ, working blacksmiths, farm animals, and much more!

Contact Info: 304 North Los Carneros Road, Goleta
(805) 964-4407
www.goletahistory.org

Santa Barbara Independence Day Celebration

Join the celebration with a host of activities. The parade makes its way down State Street followed by a patriotic rally at Chase Palm Park. The celebration finishes off with a beach party highlighted by a tremendous offshore firework show.

Contact Info: State Street, Chase Palm Park, SB Harbor
      (805) 961-2581
      www.spiritof76sb.org

Goleta Fireworks Festival

Bring your lawn chair, blanket and join the crowd for this Independence Day party.

Contact Info: Girsh Park, Goleta
      (805) 968-2773
      www.goletavalley.com

4th of July Street Fair

The Children's "Pushem-Pullem" parade starts the festivities, followed by nine blocks of artisans, food vendors, and live entertainment.

Contact Info: Main Street, Downtown Ventura
      (805)654-7830
      www.venturastreetfair.com

Santa Barbara National Horse Show

One of the most prestigious horse shows in the nation, the Santa Barbara Horse Show is the oldest horse show in the West. The program offers a variety of classes, but the kids usually enjoy the ponies most.

Contact Info: Earl Warren Showgrounds,
      3400 Calle Real Street, Santa Barbara
      (805) 687-0766
      www.earlwarren.com

French Festival

A taste of France in California – visit outdoor markets and flower stands and fresh baked pastries, sidewalk cafes with

Seasonal Festivals and Activities

checkered tablecloths. Entertainment includes over 40 acts covering 3 stages. Your kids will marvel at the puppet shows, storytellers, crepe flipping and poodle parade. The bounce house is sure to wear them out if nothing else. Bring a swimsuit and extra change of clothes for the wee ones as there is a wading pool should they choose to indulge.

Contact Info: Oak Park, Santa Barbara
　　　　　(805) 564-7274
　　　　　www.FrenchFestival.com

Santa Barbara County Fair

For over a century, this grand-daddy of local fairs has been attracting top-notch talent and entertainment. The kids will delight in the wide array of rides and games as well as the plethora of animals and live demonstrations. Food is plentiful and delicious, and the cooking and wine tasting contests are for serious contenders only. Parents will recognize the live entertainment – Pat Benatar, Kenny Loggins, and WAR all rocked the festival in 2007 alone.

Contact Info: Santa Maria Fairpark,
　　　　　937 S. Thornburg Street, Santa Maria
　　　　　(805) 925-8824
　　　　　www.santamariafairpark.com

Greek Festival

From one beautiful Riviera to another, Greece comes to Santa Barbara. Enjoy authentic Greek music and dance performances while savoring traditional Greek cuisine such as baklava, Greek summer salad, stuffed grapevine leaves, and Souvlakia. A variety of boutique shops offer imported gifts ranging from jewelry and pottery to books and music.

Contact Info: Oak Park, Santa Barbara
　　　　　(805) 683-4492
　　　　　www.saintbarbara.net

Presidio Past Times

The entire community is invited to watch the Presidio come alive as children and adults experience hands-on demonstrations and historical reenactments of early life at the Presidio, Santa Barbara's 18th century birthplace. Children get to meet the fort's uniformed soldiers (Soldados), cook delicious tortillas and make traditional hot chocolate while learning about early California foods, participate in hands-on archaeology excavations, mix and make adobe mud bricks, create ceramics, and enjoy Early California weaving and basketry demonstrations.

Contact Info: 123 E. Canon Perdido Street, Santa Barbara
(805) 965-0093
www.sbthp.org

Summer Celebration and Art Show

Summer Celebration and Art Show to Kick Off Fiesta Season at Maritime Museum.

Contact Info: SB Maritime Museum,
113 Harbor Way, Santa Barbara
(805) 962-8404
www.sbmm.org

Seasonal Festivals and Activities

August

Date	Event	Venue	Town
May–August	El Capitan Canyon Summer Concerts and BBQ	El Capitan Canyon	Santa Barbara County
May–September	Night Moves	Leadbetter Beach	Santa Barbara
May–September	Fairy Tales in the Park	Various Parks	Ventura County
June–August	Concerts in the Park	Chase Palm Park	Santa Barbara
June–October	Solvang Theaterfest	Festival Theater	Solvang
July–October	Pick Your Own Berries	Morrell Nut & Berry Farm	Solvang
August–November	Pick Your Own Apples	Apple Lane Farm	Solvang
Early August	Old Spanish Days 'Fiesta'	Santa Barbara Historical Grounds	Santa Barbara
Early August	Ventura County Fair	Seaside Park	Ventura
Mid August	Old Mission Santa Ines Fiesta	Mission Santa Ynez	Solvang
Mid August	Multicultural Dance and Music Festival	Oak Park	Santa Barbara

Mid August	Viva El Fido Mixed Breed Dog Festival	Elings Park	Santa Barbara
Late August	Dog Show	Earl Warren Showgrounds	Santa Barbara

El Capitan Canyon Summer Concerts and Barbecue

See May Section

Nite Moves

See May Section

Fairy Tales in the Park

See May Section

Concerts In The Park

See June Section

Solvang Theaterfest

See June Section

Morrell Nut & Berry Farm Pick Your Own Berries

See July Section

Apple Lane Farms

This family-owned farm graciously opens it doors every Fall for apple-picking. These apples are as good as they get, with no pesticides, just wholesome goodness. Request a recipe for their very own Apple Crisp – a true delight!

Contact Info: 1200 Alamo Pintado Road, Solvang
(805) 688-5481
www.applelanesolvang.com

Seasonal Festivals and Activities

Old Spanish Days 'Fiesta'

One of the citys' most anticipated events, this five-day celebration of Santa Barbara's Spanish heritage overflows with activity, including parades, rodeo, Mariachi Festival, El Mercado, and more. Rife with lively music and colorful Spanish dancing, La Fiesta Pequeña (The Little Fiesta) marks the official opening of Old Spanish Days on the steps of Santa Barbara's historic Old Mission. Two elaborate outdoor marketplaces, El Mercado del Norte at Mackenzie Park are abundant with Spanish and Mexican-American foods, multihued crafts, and live entertainment including children's shows. Las Noches de Ronda at the Sunken Gardens County Courthouse is a variety show of music, dances, and songs including fiery flamenco from Spain and vivid Folklórico dances from Mexico. El Desfile Histórico (Fiesta Parade) is one of the largest equestrian parades in the United States. However, the highlight for the kids is The Children's Parade on Saturday down State Street followed by the Tardes de Ronda (Children's Variety Show) at the Sunken Gardens, where kids of all age demonstrate their talents and multicultural heritage. Be sure to bring blankets and chairs for seating both for the evening Las Noches de Ronda show under the stars, as well as the parades.

Contact Info: (805) 962-8101
www.oldspanishdays-fiesta.org

Ventura County Fair

Uniquely situated directly on the beach, this "cool" venue has everything from carnival rides, agricultural exhibits to live entertainment by well known artists. Concerts are free with admission to the fair. There is something for the whole family.

Contact Info: Seaside Park, Ventura
(805) 648.3376
www.seasidepark.org

Old Mission Santa Inés Fiesta

Authentic Mexican food, Mariachi folklorico dancing and continuous entertainment highlight this celebration of the valley's rich Hispanic heritage at the Old Mission Santa Inés.

Contact Info: 1760 Mission Drive, Solvang
(805) 688-4815
www.solvangusa.com

MultiCultural Dance and Music Festival

Dance, music, storytelling, dance lessons, food and crafts from around the world.

Contact Info: Oak Park, Santa Barbara
(805) 966-6950
www.sbdancealliance.org

Viva El Fido Mixed Breed Dog Festival

Dogs of all shapes and sizes come out for a day of friendly competition in events such as Best Kisser, Highest Jumper, Best Tricks and more. Special demonstrations by the Santa Barbara Police K-9 Unit showcase their crime fighting skills and agility with their amazing speed and athleticism.

Contact Info: Elings Park, Santa Barbara
(805) 569-5611
www.elingspark.org

Dog Show

If dogs are your thing, then the 150 breeds of dogs at this show should prove to be entertaining.

Contact Info: Earl Warren Showgrounds
(323) 727-0136
www.jbradshaw.com

September

Date	Event	Venue	Town
May–September	Fairy Tales in the Park	Various Parks	Ventura County
August–November	Pick Your Own Apples	Apple Lane Farms	Solvang
Early September	Zoo-B-Q	Zoological Gardens	Santa Barbara
Mid September	Sandcastle Festival	East Beach	Santa Barbara
Mid September	Art Festival	Stow House	Santa Barbara
Mid September	Danish Days	Downtown Village	Solvang
Mid September	Old Days Festival	Downtown	Los Alamos
Mid September	Organic Festival	Alameda Park	Santa Barbara
Mid September	The Pirate Faire	Lake Casitas	Ventura
Late September	Depot Day	South Coast Railroad Museum	Goleta
Late September	SeaFest	Harbor Village	Ventura

Fairy Tales in the Park
See May Section

Apple Lane Farms
See August Section

ZOO-B-Q
Enjoy the Santa Barbara Zoo after hours at this BBQ picnic. In addition to a scrumptious BBQ dinner, there are activities for children, music, and Zookeeper presentations.

Contact Info: 500 Ninos Drive, Santa Barbara
(805) 962-5339
www.sbzoo.org

Santa Barbara Sandcastle Festival
Marvelous sandcastles and sculptures are the highlight on this day of fun in the sun at Santa Barbara's East Beach. Activities geared towards kids include treasure hunts, bounce houses, sand castle making lessons, and live music on stage. Food and refreshments provided by vendors.

Contact Info: East Beach, 1118 E Cabrillo Blvd, Santa Barbara
(805) 966-3979
www.sandcastlefestival.com

The Art Festival at Stow House
Original art by local artists, FREE admission, demos, food, crafts, live music. 10% of proceeds donated to the Goleta Valley Historical Society.

Contact Info: 302 N Los Carneros Rd., Goleta
(805) 564-7019

Solvang Danish Days

This treasured celebration of Solvang's rich Danish heritage is vivid with Old World customs and costumes. The weekend entertainment includes Danish folk dancing, music, parades, and a special Kids Corner.

Contact Info: (805) 688-6144, (800) 468-6765

www.solvangusa.com

Los Alamos Old Days Festival

Walking through Los Alamos gives you a sense of what it was like to live in an era now long past. Retaining much of its 19th century flavor, this tiny town celebrates its' history with a classic car show, peddlers mart, food booths, live entertainment, parade, dinner dance, and historical western displays.

Contact Info: Downtown, Los Alamos

(800) 230-2744

www.losalamosvalley.com

Organic Festival

The whole family will enjoy the wide variety of dynamic events offered. Parents will appreciate the brief informational lectures on creating healthy homes & gardens, and guided tours of Alice Keck Park Memorial Garden. Kids won't want to miss the children's pavilion w/ pony rides, a petting zoo, jumpers, and organic produce grown by schoolchildren. The wide array of booths offers demonstrations, arts and crafts, new inventions, and a raffle.

Contact Info: Alameda Park, 1400 Santa Barbara Street

(805) 965-4491

www.organicfestival.com

The Pirate Faire and Fall Renaissance Festival

Visitors of all ages are encouraged to come wearing a Pirate period costume. There will be costume contests both days for kids and adults alike. Enjoy pirate treasure games, and live entertainment.

Contact Info: 11311 Santa Ana Road, Ventura
(805) 649-2233
www.lakecasitas.info

Depot Day at the South Coast Railroad Museum

Depot Day commemorates and celebrates the preservation of the Goleta Depot. Enjoy a silent auction, $1 miniature train rides, music, and barbecue.

Contact Info: 300 North Los Carneros Road, Goleta
(805) 964-3540
www.goletadepot.org

Annual SeaFest

Marked by live entertainment from the moment it starts, this festival is overflowing with activity. Come partake in the interactive oceanic displays, touch tanks, hula lessons, photos with mermaids, pony rides, harbor tours and pirate magic. Marvel at the ice sculpting, World Champion Sand Sculpting and Polynesian dancing. Kids can enter the limbo contest and pedal boat races to burn off some energy.

Contact Info: 1583 Spinnaker Drive, Ventura
(805) 642-8538
www.venturaharborvillage.com

Seasonal Festivals and Activities

October

Date	Event	Venue	Town
August–November	Pick Your Own Apples	Apple Lane Farms	Solvang
October	Haunted Halloween Wagon Rides	El Capitan Ranch	Santa Barbara
October	Pumpkin Patch	Lane Farms	Goleta
October Weekends	Pumpkin Liner	Fillmore and Western Railway Co.	Fillmore
Early October	Avocado Festival	Linden Avenue	Carpinteria
Mid October	Lemon Festival	Girsh Park	Goleta
Mid October	Harbor and Seafood Festival	Harbor	Santa Barbara
Late October	Boo at the Zoo	Zoological Gardens	Santa Barbara
Late October	Heebie Jeebie Halloween	Museum of Natural History	Santa Barbara
Late October	Day in the Country	Downtown Los Olivos	Los Olivos
Late October	Childrens Costume Parade and Downtown Trick or Treat	Downtown State Street	Santa Barbara

Late October	Dia De Los Muertos Family Craft Day	Casa de la Guerra	Santa Barbara
October 31	LaCumbre Trick or Treat	LaCumbre Plaza	Santa Barbara
October 31	Ghost Village Road Trick or Treat	Coast Village Road	Montecito

Apple Lane Farms

See August Section

Haunted Halloween Wagon Rides

Listen to a colorful narration of an original tale such as The Legend of Sleepy Hollow as you travel through El Capitan Ranch on a tractor pulled wagon. Suited for all ages. Reservations required.

Contact Info: El Capitan Ranch,
10920 Calle Real, Santa Barbara
(805) 685-1147
www.elcapranch.com

Pumpkin Patch, Corn Maze, Hay Rides, etc

Harvest-themed patch has 2 1/2 acres of pumpkins ready to be picked, as well as a wide variety of other gourds to choose from. Children enjoy the horse drawn wagon rides and large corn maze. Also available are sunflowers and preserves.

Contact Info: Lane Farms,
5091 Hollister Avenue, Santa Barbara
(805) 967-1459

Seasonal Festivals and Activities

Pumpkin Liner

All Aboard! Take a train ride to the Ichabod pumpkin patch where you will enjoy activity and food booths. Search for your perfect pumpkin to bring home.

Contact Info: 351 Santa Clara Street, Fillmore
(805) 524-2546
www.fwry.com

Avocado Festival

Three days of avocado-enriched food, live music, and family fun. Head towards the Kid's Block Party where there will be activities such as games, face painting, candle making, bouncer, and avocado rock climb.

Contact Info: Linden Avenue, Carpinteria
(805) 684-5479
www.avofest.com

Goleta Lemon Festival

Touted as the biggest event in the Goleta Valley, the Lemon Festival is jam-packed with thrills for kids of all ages… pony and train rides, petting zoos, climbing walls, face painting, indy car rides, lazer tag, moon bounce and miniature golf. Don't miss Safety Street where kids get to meet the civil servants who help keep us safe and get an up-close look at their state-of-the-art vehicles.

Contact Info: Girsh Park, Goleta
(805) 967-4618
www.lemonfestival.com

Santa Barbara Harbor and Seafood Festival

Calling seafood lovers of all ages! Timed to celebrate the opening of commercial lobster season, this annual event showcases a plethora of delectable regional seafood specialties in addition to cooking demonstrations, interactive maritime education, unique children's activities, boat rides, live music, a tall-ship visit and much more.

Contact Info: Santa Barbara Harbor

(805) 897-1962

www.santabarbaraca.

gov / Visitor / Things / Waterfront

Boo at the Zoo

Enjoy traffic-free trick-or-treating during this spooktacular event. For three nights the Santa Barbara Zoo hosts a Trick & Treat Trail, Boo-Choo-Choo train rides, Creepy Crawly encounters, Spooky Storytelling, Goblin Games, nightly Costume Parades, Ghoulish Goodies and much more.

Contact Info: 500 Ninos Drive, Santa Barbara

(805) 962-5339

www.sbzoo.org

Heebie Jeebie Halloween!

AHHH! Live bats and freaky frogs greet the children at the Santa Barbara Museum of Natural History as they enjoy a costume and pie eating contests, bounces house, face painting, a planetarium show, and much more.

Contact Info: 2559 Puesta del Sol Road, Santa Barbara

(805) 682-4711

www.sbnature.org

Seasonal Festivals and Activities

Day in the Country

This beautiful Artists' community hosts an old-fashioned celebration chock full of plenty of entertainment, food and crafts.

Contact Info: Los Olivos
(805) 688-1222
www.losolivosca.com

Childrens Costume Parade and Trick-or-Treat

Calling all Goblins and Ghouls! At 11:00am before the trick-or-treating starts on State Street, a Children's Costume Parade takes place moving down State Street from Anapamu Street to De La Guerra Plaza. Come to watch or strut down the parade route by filling out a parade registration form. Trick-or-Treat along State Street between Sola and Gutierrez Streets and the Paseo Nuevo Shopping Center. Participating businesses will display an "orange ghost" and balloons in their window. Show up in costumes between 12 and 4 p.m. to receive a special treat, and don't forget to bring a Trick-or-Treat bag!

Contact Info: Downtown State Street
(805) 564-3888
www.sbpep.org

Dia de los Muertos Family Craft Day

An annual craft activity at Casa de la Guerra celebrates the history of Dia de los Muertos.

Contact Info: 9 East De la Guerra Street, Santa Barbara
(805) 965-0093
www.sbthp.org

La Cumbre Plaza Trick or Treat

Come for an early start on Halloween night. Kids can trick or treat throughout the plaza in the late afternoon.

Contact Info: 121 Hope Avenue, Santa Barbara
(805) 687-3500
www.shoplacumbre.com

Ghost Village Road

Put on your costume and come trick-or-treat on Halloween afternoon among the merchants in the upscale enclave of Montecito.

Contact Info: Coast Village Road, Montecito

November

Date	Event	Venue	Town
August – November	Pick Your Own Apples	Apple Lane Farms	Solvang
Late November	Holiday Faire	Historical Museum	Carpinteria
Late November	La Arcada Christmas Walk	La Arcada Court	Santa Barbara
Late November - December	Candy Cane Train	South Coast Railroad Museum	Goleta
Late November - December	Winterfest Celebration	Downtown Village	Solvang
Late November - December	Santa Claus Visit and Photo	LaCumbre Plaza	Santa Barbara
Late November - December	North Pole Express	Fillmore and Western Railway	Fillmore

Apple Lane Farms

See August section

Annual Holiday Faire

Carpinteria Valley Historical Museum hosts this family festival featuring arts and crafts made by over 75 artists from Central and Southern California. Children will enjoy the live music, pony rides and a visit from Santa Claus.

Contact Info: 956 Maple Avenue, Carpinteria
(805) 684-3112
www.carpinteriahistoricalmuseum.org

Annual La Arcada Court Christmas Walk

Put on a sweater and join this early evening stroll through the beautiful La Arcada Courtyard. Walk to the sounds of Carolers and Jazz musicians, and don't be surprised to find Santa there as well. Fresh popped corn and holiday treats help start the festive season.

Contact Info: 1114 State Street, Santa Barbara
(805) 962-2098
www.santabarbaradowntown.com

Candy Cane Train

Come ride the festively-decorated Candy Cane miniature train. Tickets include an assortment of holiday treats and favors, and a coupon good for a future museum train ride. Those attending the Candy Cane Train event also will be able to enjoy the museum's holiday display, Toy Trains and Teddy Bears. Hours are limited so call first. Bring a picnic lunch and take a walk to Lake Carneros from the depot.

Contact Info: 300 North Los Carneros Road, Goleta
(805) 964-3540
www.goletadepot.org

Solvang Winterfest Celebration

There is no need to travel far to experience a European Holiday. This Yule-tide celebration features a European Christmas village complete with special events, pageantry, twinkling lights and Santa Claus.

Contact Info: Downtown Solvang

(805)682-4726

www.solvangusa.com

Santa at La Cumbre Plaza

Santa arrives at LaCumbre Plaza from the North Pole on Thanksgiving Day! Come visit him anytime until Christmas. Photos are offered with Santa, which includes a special treat for the kids.

Contact Info: 121 South Hope Avenue, Santa Barbara

(805) 687-3500

www.shoplacumbre.com

North Pole Express

Bring the family dressed in pajamas for a ride to the North Pole to pick up Santa. Enjoy storytelling, caroling, cookies and milk while on board. The kids can bring their letters to Santa and mail them at the Santa's Village Post Office. Photos with Santa too! There is also another train option that features dinner with Santa.

Contact Info: 351 Santa Clara Street, Fillmore

(805)524-2546

www.fwry.com

December

Date	Event	Venue	Town
Late November - December	Candy Cane Train	South Coast Railroad Museum	Goleta
Late November - December	Winterfest Celebration	Downtown Village	Solvang
Late November - December	Santa Claus Visit and Photo	LaCumbre Plaza	Santa Barbara
Late November - December	North Pole Express	Fillmore and Western Railway	Fillmore
Early December	Holiday Parade	Downtown State Street	Santa Barbara
Early December	Christmas Patch	Lane Farms	Goleta
Early December	Holiday Party	Historical Museum	Santa Barbara
Early December	Folk and Tribal Arts Marketplace	Museum of Natural History	Santa Barbara
Early December	Christmas Parade and Tree Lighting	Linden Avenue	Carpinteria
Early December	Holiday Nature Craft Workshop	Santa Barbara Botanic Gardens	Santa Barbara
Early December	The Nutcracker	Arlington Theater	Santa Barbara

December *continued*

Date	Event	Venue	Town
Early December	The Nutcracker and Holiday Show	Lobero Theater	Santa Barbara
Early December	Christmas Parade	Downtown Village	Solvang
Early December through Christmas	Trolley of Lights	Downtown & Waterfront Santa Barbara	Santa Barbara
Early December	Olde Fashioned Christmas	Downtown	Los Olivos
Early December	Nativity Pageant	Outdoor Festival Theater	Solvang
Early December	Christmas at the Ranch	Stow House	Goleta
Early December	Parade of Lights	Channel Islands Harbor	Oxnard
Early-Mid December	Parade of Lights	Stearns Wharf	Santa Barbara
Early-Mid December	Holiday Gift-Making Workshop	Arts Alive!	Santa Barbara
Mid- December	Winter FUNderland	Museum of Natural History	Santa Barbara
Mid- December	The Nutcracker & Sugar Plum Party	Lobero Theater	Santa Barbara

Candy Cane Train

See November Section

Winterfest Celebration

See November Section

Santa at LaCumbre Plaza

See November Section

Christmas Patch

See November Section

North Pole Express

See November Section

Annual Downtown Santa Barbara Holiday Parade

Bundle up California style and join thousands of spectators lining State Street to cheer on vast groups of marching bands, expressive holiday floats, dramatic performance groups, local personalities, and the annual arrival of Santa Claus atop his festive sleigh. The Holiday Prince & Fairy christen the lighting of the large Christmas tree at State & Victoria Streets and the six smaller trees at each intersection along the parade route. The parade begins at 6:30 p.m.

Contact Info: Downtown State Street, Santa Barbara
(805) 962-2098
www.santabarbaradowntown.com

Lane Farms Christmas Patch

For a special experience picking your Christmas Tree, go to Lane Farms. Boasting five generations of farming experience in rural Goleta, this family-run farm is passionate about their patch. Try visiting during the evening as twinkling holiday lights adorn the patch and the atmosphere is ripe with holiday cheer.

Contact Info: 308 Walnut Lane, Goleta
(805) 964-3773

Annual Holiday Party

Join Father Christmas and his Court of Renaissance musicians, dancers, jugglers, and puppeteers for an evening of entertainment for the young and the young at heart at the Santa Barbara Historical Museum. A bountiful holiday buffet, wassail and boundless Yuletide cheer await.

Contact Info: 136 East De La Guerra Street, Santa Barbara
(805) 966-1601
www.santabarbaramuseum.com

Annual Folk and Tribal Arts Marketplace

Touted as the largest folk art show on California's Central Coast, this one-stop holiday gift and treasure shop at the Santa Barbara Museum of Natural History also features ethnic food and entertainment. Kids are both educated and amused by the vibrant colors and designs of the artwork brought from more than 30 adventurous dealers who have traveled the world.

Contact Info: 2559 Puesta del Sol, Santa Barbara
(805) 682-4711
www.sbnature.org

Carpinteria Holiday Parade

A Christmas parade strolls right down Linden Avenue followed by a Hospice Tree Lighting at Hollyhock Cottage.

Contact Info: Linden Avenue, Carpineteria
(805) 684-5405
www.carpchamber.org

Annual Holiday Nature Craft Workshop

Gather your family, friends, and neighbors and join the fun at the Garden's Annual Holiday Nature Craft Workshop. Make wreaths, wrapping paper, ornaments, and more, as you sip hot apple cider. This event has become a tradition at the Garden and is attended by many families year after year as a beginning to their holiday season.

Contact Info: 1212 Mission Canyon Road, Santa Barbara
(805) 682-4726
www.sbbg.org

The Nutcracker - Annual Performance

Bring the family to Santa Barbara's Only Fully Orchestrated Live Performance of The Nutcracker presented by the Santa Barbara Festival Ballet.

Contact Info: 1317 State Street, Santa Barbara
(805) 963-4408
www.sbnutcracker.com

The Nutcracker and Holiday Shows

Travel to the land of sweets with holiday classics, The Nutcracker and Twas the Night Before Christmas. Performed by dancers ages 3 and up from Gustafson Dance Studio, these shows will leave you with visions of Sugar Plums and dancing Toy Dolls.

Contact Info: Lobero Theater,
33 East Canon Perdido Street, Santa Barbara
(805) 963-0761

Solvang Christmas Parade

A hometown Christmas parade with all the trimmings completes this European-style holiday town celebration.

Seasonal Festivals and Activities

Contact Info: Downtown Solvang
                (805) 688-6144
                www.solvangusa.com

Annual Trolley of Lights

Bring the kids and enjoy hot apple cider, holiday treats, and a 90 minute lighted tour aboard the Santa Barbara trolley. This special tour is offered for two weeks in December, every evening starting around 6:30pm. Reservations are recommended.

Contact Info: Santa Barbara Trolley Company
                (805) 965-0353
                www.sbtrolley.com

Los Olivos Olde Fashioned Christmas

Local galleries and businesses host open houses as the town twinkles with hundreds of luminarias For a magical holiday experience you are invited to attend Los Olivos' "Olde Fashioned Christmas." The celebrations recreates the atmosphere of a Victorian Christmas. Santa will arrive in a horse-draw carriage to take children's Christmas wishes, local choral groups sing Christmas carols, and a "Little Angel" will light the community Christmas tree. Kids can take horse and carriage rides around the festively decorated village.

Contact Info: Downtown Los Olivos
                (805) 688-1222
                www.losolivosca.com

Solvang Nativity Pageant

Featuring a choir, traditional costumes, and live animals in Solvang's outdoor Festival Theater, this pageant is brought to you via the narration of "The Christmas Story," spoken by Efrem Zimbalist Jr.

Contact Info: Solvang Theaterfest, 420 2nd Street, Solvang
(805) 686-1789
www.solvangtheaterfest.org

Christmas at the Ranch

The historic Stow House is decorated festively for this family tradition. There are activities for the children, Santa and his reindog, a holiday boutique, music and more.

Contact Info: 304 N Los Carneros Road, Goleta
(805) 964-4407
www.GoletaHistory.org

Channel Islands Harbor Annual Parade of Lights & Festivities

The parade starts during the early evening hours, however, childrens' activities take place from 1pm-8pm.

Contact Info: 2741 South Victoria Avenue, Oxnard
(805) 985-4852
www.channelislandsharbor.org

Santa Barbara Harbor Annual Parade of Lights

Dozens of boats dress up in colorful lights and parade around the Santa Barbara Harbor while onlookers enjoy the festivities along Santa Barbara's waterfront. Santa arrives at the Harbor at 3pm escorted by the Harbor Patrol and his elves. Children come to frolic at Santa's Village, complete with 12-tons of snow from the North Pole, holiday carolers and special treats. Fireworks are an added bonus immediately after the parade.

Contact Info: Harbor & Stearns Wharf, Santa Barbara
(805) 897-1962
www.santabarbaraca.gov/Visitor/Things/
Waterfront/Annual_Parade_of_Lights

Seasonal Festivals and Activities

Holiday Gift-Making Workshop

Drop the kids off at the ARTS ALIVE! Creativity Center where they can create fun, unique, hand-made holiday gifts for their family & friends while you shop!

Contact Info: 1 N. Calle Cesar Chavez, Suite 100
(805) 963-2278
www.artsalivesb.com

Winter FUNderland

A snow day in Santa Barbara! Santa, Frosty, holiday reindeer and other winter animals are the center of attraction for the kids at the Santa Barbara Museum of Natural History. Experience winter crafts, stories, and the magical planetarium show "Santa's Starry Ride." Don't forget your camera!

Contact Info: 2559 Puesta del Sol, Santa Barbara
(805) 682-4711
www.sbnature.org

The Nutcracker

A holiday tradition for everyone! State Street Ballet presents this Sunday matinee followed by the Sugar Plum Party for children (tickets available separately). Enjoy crafts, entertainment, goodies and more. Kids especially enjoy taking their photo with the Sugar Plum Fairy.

Contact Info: Lobero Theatre
(805) 687-6086
www.lobero.com

Day and Overnight Trips from Santa Barbara

Day Trips

NORTH OF SANTA BARBARA

SANTA YNEZ VALLEY

Cachuma Lake Recreation Area

Cachuma Lake is renowned for its natural beauty and variety of fun things to do. Children's playgrounds, lake cruises, the nature center, fishing piers, and hiking trails await you and your family. Bring BBQ fixings and use one of the grills in the park alongside the lake. Call their Nature Center for information about their special events such as Kids Fishing Workshops, Kids Learn Birds, and Astronomy Nights. Consider staying overnight in their Yurts.

Contact Info: HC 59 - Highway 154 , Santa Barbara
(805) 686-5054
www.cachuma.com

Quicksilver Miniature Horse Ranch

While this breeding facility does not offer petting pens, children are able to get up close and personal with the miniature horses.

Contact Info: 1555 Alamo Pintado Road, Solvang

(805) 686-4002

www.syv.com/qsminis/

Clairmont Farms

This family owned lavender farm welcomes visitors to stroll through the fields, and picnic and shop in their boutique. Tours take place each day.

Contact Info: 2480 Roblar Street, Los Olivos

(805) 688 7505

www.clairmontfarms.com

Ostrich Land

Kids can feed and come face to face with an Ostrich on this farm. There is also a gift store with novelty items such as empty ostrich egg shells, ostrich jerky, and ostrich feather key rings.

Contact Info: 610 E. Highway 246, Buellton

(805) 686-9696

www.ostrichlandusa.com

Elverhoj Museum of History and Art

The Kid's Saturday Morning Art series are popular as they explore a variety of art mediums, with something new for each class. Some kids are fascinated by the meticulously detailed miniature scaled models of Danish buildings from the first 20 years of Solvang. Ask for the Kids Scavenger Hunt and the Viking Alphabet word puzzle.

Contact Info: 1624 Elverhoy Way, Solvang
(805) 686-1211
www.elverhoj.org

Hans Christian Anderson Museum

The Hans Christian Andersen Museum is operated by the Ugly Duckling Foundation, a non profit organization established to foster public understanding and enjoyment of Hans Christian Andersen and his work.

Contact Info: 1680 Mission Drive, Solvang
(805) 688-2052
www.bookloftsolvang.com / museum

Solvang Vintage Motorcycle Museum

If wheels are your kids obsession, then come set your eyes on this private motorcycle collection of vintage and rare motor-cycles as well as European race bikes.

Contact Info: 320 Alisal Road, Solvang
(805) 686-9522
www.motosolvang.com

The Wildling Art Museum

Dedicated to presenting the art of America's wilderness, this educational institution focuses on the goal that kids of all ages gain a greater appreciation of art and a better understanding of the importance of preserving our natural heritage.

Contact Info: 2329 Jonata Street, Los Olivos – (805)688-1082
www.wildlingmuseum.org

SANTA MARIA

Santa Maria Valley Discovery Museum

Fun, hands-on activities for kids of all ages, from toddlers up.

Contact Info: 705 McClelland, Santa Maria
(805) 928-8414
www.smvdiscoverymuseum.org

Santa Maria Museum of Flight

Established in 1988, this museum is located on an old air base.

Contact Info: 3015 Airpark Drive, Santa Maria
(805) 922-8758
www.smmof.org

Santa Maria Speedway

This small, unpretentious Speedway is nestled in a semi-amphitheater of natural terrain, sheltered by dense eucalyptus trees. Stock cars, Sprint cars… you name it. Kids can't get enough of the roar of the engine and the pedal to the metal. Call for hours, specific race information, and directions.

Contact Info: (805) 466-4462
www.santamariaspeedway.com

The Dunes Center

Quaint museum with interactive exhibits for kids: Chumash Indians exhibit, puppets on stage, shells & magnifying glasses, interactive computers, and a sandbox.

Contact Info: Guadalupe Street, Guadalupe
(805) 343-2455

SOUTH OF SANTA BARBARA
VENTURA

Ventura Harbor Village

Stroll along the waterfront Promenade and peruse the many gift shops, including the kite store which boasts the largest selection of kites in the county. A colorful carousel sits surrounded by shops, and the Swift of Ipswich wooden pirate ship is open to the public for tours. Rent a paddle boat and cruise the harbor.

Contact Info: 1559 Spinnaker Drive, Ventura
(805) 644-0169
www.VenturaHarborVillage.com

Channel Island Visitors Center

Near the Harbor, sits the Channel Islands Visitors Center. The center has a museum, a bookstore, a three-story observation tower with telescopes, and island exhibits. There is a living tide pool display and full-size reproductions of a male northern elephant seal and the pygmy mammoth skeleton unearthed on Santa Rosa Island in 1994.

Contact Info: 1901 Spinnaker Dr., Ventura
(805) 658-5730
www.nps.gov/archive/chis/hqpage.htm

Casitas Water Adventure

This Water Wonderland is divided into water playgrounds for different age levels, including toddlers. There is something for everyone from jungle gyms, waterfalls, bridges and slides, to an inner tube ride down the Lazy River. Be sure to bring a beach umbrella or two in case you don't find a lounge chair in a shaded area. Open mid-May to September.

Contact Info: 11311 Santa Ana Road, Ventura
(805) 649-2233, (805) 649-1122
www.lakecasitas.info

Golf N' Stuff

A family fun park with 2 creatively landscaped miniature golf courses, a lit'l indy raceway, ram rod bumper cars, wet and wild bumper boats, lazer tag arena, an arcade, and a full snack bar facility.

Contact Info: 5555 Walker Street, Ventura
(805) 644-7131
www.golfnstuff.com

Adventures for Kids

This whimsical childrens bookstore also sells games, toys, music, and much, much more. Story times are held twice a week.

Contact Info: 3457 Telegraph Road, Ventura
(805)650-9688
www.adventuresforkids.com

OXNARD

Channel Islands Harbor

This harbor is filled with things to do – from shopping and dining to beaches and boating. The large visitor's center has models and photographs of the Channel Islands, nature exhibits, and touchable tide pools. Hop on the water taxi for a short excursion or try out a whale watching tour. Check out the events calendar on the web site for seasonal and educational events. From Fairytales in the Park to 3-Hour Cannon Battle Reenactment Sail Tours, there is always something exciting for the whole family.

Contact Info: 2741 South Victoria Avenue, Suite F, Oxnard
(805) 985-4852
www.channelislandsharbor.org

Gull Wings Childrens Museum

This climb-on, try-out museum includes more than 15 engaging exhibits, many focused on the California coast. Kids can captain a ship, explore sea life touch tanks, or visit the farmers market. Only three blocks away from the Amtrak station, try taking the train from Santa Barbara down to Oxnard for a complete adventure. Call for hours as they are closed many holidays and Sundays.

Contact Info: 418 W. 4th Street, Oxnard
(805) 483-3005
www.gullwings.org

FILLMORE & ALONG HWY 126

Fillmore & Western Railway Co.

Restored vintage trains offering weekend scenic excursions as well as special events such as: Dinner with Santa, Christmas Tree Trains, Pumpkin Liners, North Pole Express, Day Out With Thomas™, and many more.

Contact Info: 250 Central Ave, Fillmore
(800) 773-8724
www.fwry.com

Six Flags Magic Mountain & Hurricane Harbor

Known world wide as a thrill ride haven, Six Flags Magic Mountain features 15 world-class roller coasters. Next door, set amidst the fringes of a tropical jungle, Hurricane Harbor is a 12-acre water park featuring two of the tallest fully enclosed speed slides in Southern California. Best suited for older kids.

Contact Info: 26101 Magic Mountain Parkway, Valencia

(661) 255-4100

www.sixflags.com

MOORPARK

Americas Teaching Zoo, Moorpark College.

Moorpark College hosts the Exotic Animal Training and Management Program. Every weekend, Americas Teaching Zoo is open to the public. You can explore the zoo, watch feedings, and attend 15-minute demonstrations.

Contact Info: 7075 Campus Road, Moorpark

(805) 378-1441

www.moorpark.cc.ca.us/~eatm/

Underwood Family Farms

Bring the entire family for a fun, educational day "out on the farm". Pick fresh fruits and vegetables, pet and feed the animals, and enjoy pony rides and a bounce house. Pull-wagons are provided so that the kids can haul their own prize pickings.

Contact Info 3370 Sunset Valley Road, Moorpark

(805) 529-3690

www.underwoodfamilyfarms.com

Overnight Trips

. . . .

LOS ANGELES

Page Museum - La Brea Tar Pits

Rancho La Brea is one of the world's most famous fossil localities, recognized for having the largest and most diverse assemblage of extinct Ice Age plants and animals in the world.

Contact Info: 5801 Wilshire Boulevard, Los Angeles
(323) 934-7243
www.tarpits.org

Universal Studios

Spend a day at this theme park that's as fun for grown-ups as it is for kids. Kids can meet their favorite characters... SpongeBob SquarePants, Dora the Explorer, Shrek, Spider-Man, and more. Witness the world's smartest trained animal performers in Universal's Animal Actors. Join the water fun in the Nickelodeon® Blast Zone.

Contact Info: 100 Universal City Plaza, Universal City
(818) 622-1111
www.universalstudioshollywood.com

California Science Center

Touted as the West Coast's largest hands-on science center, the California Science Center offers fun and informative exhibits presented in interactive worlds.

Contact Info: 700 State Drive, Los Angeles
(323) 724-3623
www.californiasciencecenter.org

KidSpace Children Museum

Programs and exhibits in the arts, sciences and humanities promote investigation, exploration and expression for children ages 1 to 9.

Contact Info: 480 North Arroyo Blvd, Pasadena
(626) 449-9144
www.kidspacemuseum.org

J. Paul Getty Museum

An exquisite museum hosting a special Family Room, filled with educational and hands-on activities. Family tours feature fun, activity-filled visits to the galleries. In addition, special seasonal programs are designed to engage the whole family.

Contact Info: 1200 Getty Center Drive, Los Angeles
(310) 440-7300
www.getty.edu

Aquarium of the Pacific

Encounter more than 12,500 animals as you explore sunny Southern California and Baja, the frigid waters of the North Pacific, and the colorful reefs of the Tropical Pacific. Children enjoy the hands-on exhibits, playground, and shows – don't miss the seals and sea lions! Of course, the ultimate experience is coming face-to-face with, and even touching, the ocean's legendary predators in Shark Lagoon.

Contact Info: 100 Aquarium Way, Long Beach 90802
(562) 590-3100
www.aquariumofpacific.org

Santa Monica Pier

The finish line of famed Route 66, the Santa Monica Pier is a recreational and entertainment venue. In addition to an aquarium, there is a whole amusement park on the grounds, with rides for every age.

Contact Info: 1600 Ocean Front Walk, Santa Monica
(310)393-6149
www.santamonicapier.org
www.pacpark.com

ORANGE COUNTY

Disneyland Park and Resort:

The Amtrak train from Santa Barbara will take you directly to Disneyland Resort where you can enjoy a day or two taking in all the amusements. You will not need a car there. Besides the amusement park, the attractions include the adjacent Disney Grand California Hotel and an entire village of restaurants, shopping, and movie theaters called Downtown Disney District.

Contact Info: 1313 S. Harbor Blvd., Anaheim
(714) 781-4565
www.disneyland.com

Knotts Berry Farm

From Camp Snoopy to roller coasters, there are rides and attractions for every age level at "America's First Theme Park". Don't skip the famous fried chicken on your visit.

Contact Info: 8039 Beach Boulevard, Buena Park
(714) 220-5200
www.knotts.com

Medieval Times Dinner and Tournament

While at Disneyland or Knotts, consider a visit to the Medieval Times Castle, just a few minutes away, for an extravagant feast and show, complete with jousting. Guests receive a colored crown corresponding to their seating area and the Knight they will cheer throughout the show.

Contact Info: 7662 Beach Blvd, Buena Park

(888) We-Joust

www.medievaltimes.com

SAN LUIS OBISPO

Avila Beach Boardwalk

This hidden seaside gem is home to a lively boardwalk along a picturesque Avila Beach. Take a short stroll with the kids while enjoying a snow cone and hot dog. The wee pirate will delight in the ocean-themed play area at the end of the boardwalk, complete with a ship and lookout mast. On your way, don't miss the **Avila Valley Barn** – a Farmers Market including a petting zoo with ponies, donkeys, pigs, goats, sheep and more barnyard animals. Hay rides are offered on weekends also – Open seasonally – call for hours (805)595-2810 or visit www.avilavalleybarn.com

Contact Info: Avila Beach Drive, San Luis Obispo

(805) 595-2810

www.visitavilabeach.com

Hearst Castle

Home to 165 rooms and 127 acres of gardens, terraces, pools and walkways, this seaside estate is spectacular with a fascinating history. Try to view the large format informational movie at the visitors center first, at least as long as your kids can sit through it. Adults with small children may find the stairs and museum restrictions challenging. Strollers are not permitted.

Contact Info: 750 Hearst Castle Road, San Simeon

(800) 444-4445

www.hearstcastle.com

Montana de Oro State Park.

From beautiful coved beaches to sheer cliffs, eucalyptus groves, streams, tide pools, and an abundance of natural wildlife, Montana De Oro is a scenic masterpiece. The tide pools at Hazards Beach are well worth a visit – visit during a low tide.

Contact Info: 1 Pecho Valley Road, Los Osos
(805) 772-7434
www.slostateparks.com/montana_de_oro

Museum of Natural History in Morro Bay

This small museum has interactive exhibits for kids of all ages.

Contact Info: Morro Bay State Park Road, Morro Bay
(805) 772-2694
www.ccnha.org

Lake Lopez Mustang Water Slides

Nestled in oak-studded hills, the Mustang Water Slides, Pony Pools, and Stampede half-pipe are sure to cool you off on a hot day. There are also mini-slides, wading pools, and umbrella showers for the wee ones. While you're here be sure to visit Doc Burnstein's Ice Cream Lab in the nostalgic Old Town Arroyo Grande.

Contact Info: Lopez Lake Recreation Area, Arroyo Grande
(805)489-8898
(805)489-8832 reservations
www.mustangwaterslides.com

Charles Paddock Zoo

Set in beautiful Atascadero Lake Park, this small community zoo features over 100 animals on 5 acres of land. Come see unique species such as the rare Indo-Chinese Tigers and curious Spider Monkeys. Enjoy the nearby lake on your way out.

Hours: 10am-5pm

Contact Info: 9305 Pismo Avenue, Atascadero
(805) 461-5080
www.charlespaddockzoo.org

San Luis Obispo Childrens Museum

An aesthetically modern and well lit "town square" setting, this museum features hands-on exhibits for toddlers to pre-teens. The central location makes it a convenient stop for those looking to also explore downtown San Luis Obispo. Please call for hours first as the museum has been under construction.

Contact Info: 1108 Garden St., Ste. 212, San Luis Obispo
(805) 545-5874
www.slokids.org

Local Web Resources

Local Santa Barbara News and Events

www.tixity.com

www.edhat.com

www.independent.com

www.santabarbaradowntown.com

www.santabarbaraca.com

www.sbfamilylife.com

www.santabarbara.com

Chamber of Commerce & Visitor Information

www.sbchamber.org - **Santa Barbara**

www.carpchamber.org - **Carpinteria**

www.goletavalley.com - **Goleta**

www.syvva.com - **Santa Ynez Valley**

www.ojaichamber.org - **Ojai Valley**

www.ventura-chamber.org – **Ventura**

www.oxnardchamber.org - **Oxnard**

The Great Santa Barbara Outdoors

www.sbbike.org

www.sb-outdoors.com

www.santabarbarahikes.com

An exceptional resource for parents in Santa Barbara

www.sbparent.com

Index

Index

Index

T
. . . .

U
. . . .

V
. . . .

W
. . . .

Z
. . . .

Index

Photo Courtesy of Elizabeth Peace Photography

About the Author

Annabelle Abba Brownell is married with two children and the founder of Santa Barbara Baby Company, an infant and toddler equipment rental company. It is a service -based company with an online storefront. In the time that she isn't exploring Santa Barbara with her own family, she advises her visiting clients on the best choices for experiencing Santa Barbara with their kids.

Prior to moving to Santa Barbara, Ms. Brownell lived and worked in the Silicon Valley for over a decade. She made a career of joining companies experiencing rapid growth. She successfully built out several marketing organizations at high-tech start-up companies and was instrumental in the efforts to expand their channel and online presence.

Ms. Brownell holds an MBA from Thunderbird School of Global Management and a BA from UCLA.